We as parents cannot impart what  We can issue our children lots of ou dos, but in the end they won't ring true if haven't yet transformed *us*. In his latest book, *Raising a Child Who Prays*, Dr. David Ireland not only equips you to pray, but he also teaches you to teach your children to pray. Jesus loves children. His promises are as true for them as they are for us. What might change in our families today, and in the world at large, if more and more children—with their childlike faith still intact—learned how to pray God's promises? I love this line from Dr. Ireland's book: "Prayer gives our kids access to God's limitless authority." Amen. Read and apply the words on these pages. Then marvel as God begins to move mightily in and through your children.

—Susie Larson
National Speaker, Talk Radio Host, and
Author, *Your Powerful Prayers*

I have tremendous respect and admiration for David Ireland, a brilliant, strategic leader and a man of deep, godly character. David is articulate and passionate and an all-around great guy! So, when I heard he was releasing a new book titled *Raising a Child Who Prays*, I knew it would be funny, insightful, practical, and helpful. This book is filled with heartwarming stories that emphasize the importance of teaching children about faith and relationship with the One who loves them most! You will absolutely love this book, and I highly recommend it for every parent and grandparent seeking to lead little ones to Jesus.

—Santiago "Jimmy" Mellado
President and CEO, Compassion International
Coauthor, *Small Matters*

With so many books on parenting flooding the market-place, it is refreshing to find one that promises—and then delivers—practical, tangible instruction and insight that can make a genuine, lifelong impact on Christian families. *Raising a Child Who Prays* is such a book. Chapter by chapter David Ireland unfolds powerful tools parents can use right away to help their children establish a vibrant and consistent pattern of coming before the throne of grace. You cannot read this book without being challenged in your thinking about the importance of teaching your children and grandchildren to pray, no matter how young they are. *Raising a Child Who Prays* should be mandatory reading for Christian parents.

—MICHAEL G. SCALES, EdD
PRESIDENT, NYACK COLLEGE AND ALLIANCE
THEOLOGICAL SEMINARY

I wish I could have had this book as a resource when my children were young and I was attempting to rear them to grow up knowing God. I knew as a parent that modeling and living my Christian experience before them was of utmost importance. I modeled before them a prayer life, prayed for and with them, but would have appreciated the directions Dr. Ireland gives in this book for raising them to pray at an early age. I would encourage Christian parents to use this book as a guide to teaching the whole family the power of prayer.

—DR. FREDA V. CREWS
HOST, *TIME FOR HOPE*,
AN INTERNATIONAL, FAITH-BASED
MENTAL HEALTH TV PROGRAM

This is an amazing book. Extraordinary. Profound. Sobering. Encouraging. I only wish I had access to it as our own children were growing up. I urge every parent to read it carefully and prayerfully. It will change your life—and your child's.

—DR. R. T. KENDALL
MINISTER, WESTMINSTER CHAPEL (1977–2002)

Written through the lens of a father's heart, *Raising a Child Who Prays* offers practical, relevant, and biblically rich insight to inspire the heart of our children toward their most valuable tool in life—prayer. Prayer is the epicenter of one's spiritual walk regardless of age, and David Ireland's book creates a ripple in the family framework of parenting that is sure to build, form, and disciple young prayer warriors in this generation and beyond. It is undeniably the most important book every parent will read as they endeavor to set the course of their child's spiritual development.

—SERGIO DE LA MORA
LEAD PASTOR, CORNERSTONE CHURCH OF SAN DIEGO
AUTHOR, *THE HEART REVOLUTION*

Having heard Dr. Ireland teach on prayer and then lead hundreds of men on their faces before God—me included—it was clear: he knew his way around God's throne room.

—PASTOR TOMMY BARNETT
AUTHOR
SENIOR PASTOR, PHOENIX FIRST ASSEMBLY OF GOD
CHANCELLOR, SOUTHEASTERN UNIVERSITY

Dr. David Ireland is an amazing apostolic gift with such a prolific mind. His gift is displayed in what he has built and established and maintained. There are those who haven't built anything and cannot teach "it." There are those who teach "it" but haven't built anything. There are those who have built "it" and can't teach "it"; but there are those who have built "it" and teach "it." David Ireland has built "it" and is teaching "it." God has raised him to teach this generation how to war through prayer.

—BISHOP TUDOR BISMARK
JABULA NEW LIFE MINISTRIES
HARARE, ZIMBABWE

God uses David Ireland to communicate His Word with unusual passion and the anointing of the Holy Spirit.

—JIM CYMBALA
AUTHOR
SENIOR PASTOR, THE BROOKLYN TABERNACLE

Every teaching of Dr. Ireland gives you the detail and wisdom of a PhD, and also the love and compassion of a child.

—KURT WARNER
RETIRED NFL QUARTERBACK

When Concerts of Prayer Greater New York desires to display an awesome praying pastor, we often point to Pastor David Ireland of Christ Church. He models prayer and boldly leads his congregation through main prayer disciplines that are often neglected. Dr. David Ireland is a significant leader in the body of Christ.

—DIMAS SALABERRIOS
PRESIDENT, CONCERTS OF PRAYER
GREATER NEW YORK

I remember meeting Dr. David Ireland for the first time almost two decades ago and saying to myself—that is a smart, Jesus-loving, highly organized, and gifted communicator of the gospel and leadership. Dr. Ireland's very diverse academic preparation as an engineer as well as a theologian allows him to do biblical architecture with complex issues of the Scripture. He's a man of integrity and obvious passion. He will bless, challenge, and encourage you regardless of the context. I highly recommend my friend Dr. David Ireland.

—Dr. Samuel R. Chand
Author, *Leadership Pain:
The Classroom for Growth*

Raising a
CHILD
WHO
PRAYS

Raising a
CHILD
WHO
PRAYS

---◦---

DAVID D. IRELAND, PhD

CHARISMA
HOUSE

Most CHARISMA HOUSE BOOK GROUP products are available at special quantity discounts for bulk purchase for sales promotions, premiums, fund-raising, and educational needs. For details, write Charisma House Book Group, 600 Rinehart Road, Lake Mary, Florida 32746, or telephone (407) 333-0600.

RAISING A CHILD WHO PRAYS by David D. Ireland, PhD
Published by Charisma House
Charisma Media/Charisma House Book Group
600 Rinehart Road
Lake Mary, Florida 32746
www.charismahouse.com

Cover design by Studio Gearbox
Design Director: Justin Evans

Visit the author's website at www.DavidIreland.org.

Library of Congress Cataloging-in-Publication Data:
An application to register this book for cataloging has been submitted to the Library of Congress.
International Standard Book Number: 978-1-62998-945-7
E-book ISBN: 978-1-62998-946-4

This publication is translated in Spanish under the title *Cómo criar niños que oran*, copyright © 2016 by David D. Ireland, published by Casa Creación, a Charisma Media company. All rights reserved.

publisher nor the author assumes any responsibility for errors or for changes that occur after publication.

First edition

16 17 18 19 20 — 9 8 7 6 5 4 3 2 1

Printed in the United States of America

*To my mother, Sylvia Ireland, who
instilled in me the love of books
while teaching me how to write.*

———————— ☼ ————————

TABLE OF CONTENTS

———— ☼ ————

Foreword *by Dr. Wess Stafford* xvii

Introduction xxi

Chapter 1   The Power of a Praying Parent 1

Chapter 2   The Power of a Praying Child 17

Chapter 3   Jesus—the First Twelve Years 37

Chapter 4   Little Johnny (a.k.a. John the Baptist) . . . 53

Chapter 5   Unlocking Kid Power 71

Chapter 6   Add Faith to Your Prayers 91

Chapter 7   Praying God's Dream for Your Child . . . 109

Chapter 8   Help, God! 129

Chapter 9   God, Are You OK? 147

Conclusion 165

Appendix: Prayer Exercises 169

Notes 183

FOREWORD

———— ☼ ————

IN FOUR DECADES of international ministry to children I have heard the prayers of many thousands of children in dozens of languages and am convinced there is no greater power on earth—children have a hotline to heaven! Simple and inarticulate as the prayer of a child may be, it goes straight to the heart of God. Matthew 18:10 records that Jesus said: "Beware that you don't look down upon a single one of these little children. For I tell you that in heaven their angels have constant access to my Father" (TLB). As Dr. David Ireland reminds us, God listens to hearts, not words. The innocence and sincerity of children and their utter faith and courage to believe and ask anything grips God's heart—"of such is the kingdom of heaven" (Matt. 19:14, NKJV). A surprise awaits us in heaven when we discover that it was very often the prayers of children that moved heaven and earth!

As with other life skills we impart to our sons and daughters, the time to teach the discipline of prayer is in childhood, as soon as little ones can lisp a prayer. In Psalm 8:2 David suggests prayers of praise begin with a baby's first happy coos. "Nursing infants gurgle choruses about you; toddlers shout the songs that drown out enemy talk" (THE MESSAGE). Prayer is both an *invitation* from God Almighty—"Call to Me, and I will answer you, and show you great and mighty things, which you do not know" (Jer. 33:3, NKJV)—and a *mandate*—"Pray without ceasing" (1 Thess. 5:17, NKJV). From womb to tomb it is our greatest privilege to be in constant communion with our God.

In this important book my friend Dr. David Ireland challenges us parents: What better spiritual legacy could we leave to our children than a strong prayer life? What could be more important than for them to learn how to hear from God? Prayer shapes their hearts, builds faith, deepens character, develops compassion for others, teaches gratitude and praise, and fosters spiritual maturity. And should they wander from walking with God later in life, it establishes a familiar pathway back home to the waiting arms of their loving Savior.

It is tempting, in light of this huge responsibility to teach our children to pray, to feel woefully inadequate. We may think, "Nobody taught me," or "I'm not much of a prayer warrior myself." But the fact that you have picked up this book speaks volumes about the desires of your good heart and your deep love for your children and their spiritual formation. By the way, be prepared to be blessed by how much the process of teaching your child to pray revolutionizes your own prayer life!

The joyful privilege and sacred duty of teaching our children to pray is crucial and very doable. This book is a detailed road map that is both inspirational and practical, written by a man of prayer. Similar to him, it is warm, humorous, and insightful. May your heart be stirred and rewarded as you begin to hear from the lips of your child, "I pray this in Jesus's name, amen."

—Dr. Wess Stafford
President Emeritus, Compassion International
Author, *Too Small to Ignore:
Why the Least of These Matters Most*
and *Just a Minute: In the Heart of a Child,
One Moment...Can Last Forever*

INTRODUCTION

———— ✹ ————

I WAS NOT EXPECTING this. My plan was to spend a few minutes in the prayer room after a global conference in South Korea. The room was humming with the sound of small voices.

"God, give me Mexico!" came the plea from a corner of the prayer room. Another voice sobbed, "Lord, send me to Pakistan!" In the same moment I heard a third voice coming from a tiny prostrate figure cry, "Use me in Turkey."

When I looked to see who was praying, my knees buckled as they hit the floor. My eyes flooded with tears. Instead of the customary die-hard intercessors, I was shocked to see little children—some as young as seven years old. Since it was nighttime, the kids had on their pajamas. One was fitted with Superman-looking nightwear; another looked like a little princess. But they were all eagerly seeking the Lord. The image of these pint-sized intercessors crying out before God became etched in my mind. It was *their* little voices that pleaded for Mexico, Pakistan, and Turkey.

I could hardly concentrate on my own prayers because my mind was racing a million miles a minute. These little kneeling warriors had exposed my ignorance about kids and prayer. My preconceived notions of chronological age and spiritual growth were being debunked—no, decimated. These children *knew how to pray*. They knew how to plead their cases before God's throne of grace. There was no doubt; God's throne room was just as accessible to His little subjects as it was to the adults in His kingdom.

These missionary kids were not asking God for a comfortable, middle-class life. They weren't even asking for the latest electronic gadget—or an old version, for that matter. As I drew near, I felt their heart after God. These kids knew the power and necessity of prayer. Their parents lived on the front lines of Christianity. Some were stationed in countries with strict laws forbidding the propagation of Christianity. In fact, some of these nations have religious and cultural views that hold Christianity so objectionable that imprisonment or death awaits its followers. Despite the difficulty of living for Christ, these children were asking God to send them to dangerous places to serve.

I thought to myself, "If every parent could see and understand the power of praying kids, they would pay far more attention to their children's spiritual development." The fact that this book is in your hands speaks volumes about you. You care! You are convinced that your kids can learn how to pray. And you're absolutely correct. Read on. I will teach you how to raise a child (or grandchild) who prays. It's vital to attaining a flourishing Christian life.

Although your kids will learn how to pray, they will still be kids. Sometimes cute prayers will emerge from their mouths because they are kids. One kid prayed:

> Dear God, please take care of my daddy and my mommy and my sister and my brother and my doggy and me. Oh, please take care of Yourself, God. If anything happens to You, we're gonna be in a big mess.

Despite these laughable moments there will be serious ones that let us know they are just as connected with God as we are. Your kids can learn how to pray. They just need some guidance and patience. That is where you come in.

WHY I WROTE THIS BOOK

My wife and I are pastors who have served in ministry for nearly thirty years. But even as pastors, when Marlinda and I were teaching our now-grown daughters to pray, we could have used some help. Sometimes our coaching was almost perfect—textbook perfect. Other times it wasn't pretty. Our kids were resistant. My methods were weak and boring. Our attitudes were less than stellar, to say the least. It looked like an un-fixable train wreck.

Tears, heavy hearts, and sullen faces were the family portrait during those moments. Yet if you take to heart Jesus's perspective that we "should always pray and not give up" (Luke 18:1, NIV), even during tough times God will show Himself faithful on your behalf. Just don't quit! Parenting is a marathon and not a sixty-yard dash.

Over my years in the pastorate I have observed children praying with fervency and passion. These intercessors always had a parent who encouraged them that they matter to God. Raising a child who prays is very much doable, even in our fast-paced and broken culture. As you learn to rely on the Lord and His grace, you will discover wisdom from above that will guide you throughout the many seasons of your parental life. You're not on your own. God is with you. And your child will follow suit as you stay the course.

According to the International Bible Society, nearly 85 percent of people who become Christ-followers do so between the age of four and fourteen.[1] In fact, this statistical data is now known as the 4/14 Window. Christian organizations are creating and pouring resources into ministry to children within that age group because of the tremendous results it yields.

If Christianity is to maintain its global presence to future generations, we must place a heavy emphasis on the spiritual development of our children. It's not good enough for us to have a strong spiritual life while our kids coast along in neutral. Our children must also enjoy a rich spiritual life. True Christianity is apparent when your life is filled with fire and zeal for the Lord. This only comes from the fuel of prayer.

I wrote this book as a parental guide. I want to come alongside you to demystify prayer, encourage you, and provide helpful how-to tips as you raise your children to pray. This is a coachable skill, just as all the other stages of parenting. Remember back to the days of potty training and shoelace tying? Or even bigger feats, such as teaching them to share or say "thank you"? You successfully climbed those mountains. If you're still scaling those peaks, climb on. Victory is ahead. It's sweet.

THE BOOK'S BENEFITS

There are quite a number of books on the market telling us of the need to teach our children about prayer, but very few tell you *how*. This book offers three benefits.

Provides prayer-coaching tips

I am going to serve as your prayer coach throughout the book. I will offer encouragement and instruction in such an accessible way that it will build your confidence and feed your own spiritual growth. This is critical because you are your child's first and most memorable teacher. If your prayer life grows deeper and more mature, you'll be more successful in raising a praying child. It's only logical for you to develop a healthy prayer life before you can ask someone else to do the same. If you find no personal benefit to prayer, neither will your children. The best sermon is a lived sermon.

Sharing the value and relevance of prayer will only resonate with your kids after they have seen answers to prayer firsthand. Don't worry; you'll have tons of answers. God is a prayer-answering God. He doesn't get glory out of unanswered prayers. It's just the opposite. God gets glory out of *answered* prayers. Similar to any other parent, God delights when His children can say: "The LORD is my shepherd, I shall not want" (Ps. 23:1). Answered prayers cause us to not be in want.

There are short prayers within each lesson and at the conclusion of each chapter I invite you to pray. At the end of the book there are practical prayer exercises that you and your child can do together. They are fun, relevant to the culture in which we live, and quite instructional. This keeps the book practical while giving you an opportunity to watch God answer your prayers.

Highlights praying kids

Raising a Child Who Prays will help you understand that God does not push the pause button on your children's spiritual life and wait until they're adults. His throne room is accessible to them. This you will see as I unpack the spiritual development and steps praying kids (in the Bible and present day) took to experience a rich prayer life.

Each chapter is packed with funny stories and simple techniques to help your child learn how to pray. You will hear from parents just like you who have successfully raised tiny kneeling warriors.

Raising a Child Who Prays will help to answer the following questions:

- What do I need to grow spiritually and be a better role model?

- How can I pray for my kids more effectively?

- How do children develop spiritually?

- How can I teach my kids how to pray?

- What does a healthy prayer life look like for a child?

- How can I make sure my prayer lessons will grow with them?

Provides parenting tips

Throughout the book I will offer information that will help you understand the emotional, psychological, and spiritual development of children. Understanding the social science behind the spiritual formation of kids and how they process religious truths will be invaluable to raising a child who prays. This kind of information makes your parenting holistic.

Raising a Child Who Prays hones in on the practical side of parenting. God has great plans for your children. Raising them with the life skill of prayer is essential for them to accomplish those God-inspired plans. We cannot ignore this aspect of parenting.

Thousands of years ago Jeremiah the prophet bellowed: "'For I know the plans I have for you,' declares the LORD, 'plans to prosper you and not to harm you, plans to give you hope and a future'" (Jer. 29:11, NIV). These words are alive today. They speak of God's dream for you and for your children.

Your child is destined for greatness! These are not simply the encouraging words of a writer, but God's word found in the sacred Scriptures. *Raising a Child Who Prays* will help see to it that God's dreams for your children are fulfilled.

THE POWER OF A
PRAYING PARENT

———— ❖ ————

I WAS JUST TWELVE years old. I had never before seen anyone so sick. My paternal grandfather was on his deathbed. The left side of his body was paralyzed from a severe stroke. Unable to speak, he pointed to the nearby chest of drawers with his one functioning arm. Four black Bibles were stacked one on top of the other. The nurse brought them over. Apparently he wanted to be the one who gave the books to each of his grandkids. By birth order my siblings and I each walked up to his bedside. I was the third.

I was terribly frightened. Up-close and personal, death looked nothing like it did on television. His vacant, ashen face had lost its natural, vibrant brown color. His eyes were gray and murky looking. I slowly approached him, trying to stall as long as possible. I was really scared. I remember my dad nudging me forward by putting his open hand in the center of my back. I resisted a little, but his strength proved too much to battle. His discreet shove swiftly moved me to the bedside of *his* father.

With his right hand my grandfather handed me his treasured gift. He could speak only through expressions from his clouded eyes and strained facial movements. I don't think I'd ever seen a Bible before that day, nor did I have a frame of reference—or reverence—for what it meant. The heavy, leather-bound bundle of pages was clearly very important to him. But to me, it was just a book—a black, hardcover book. He died a few days later.

I was somewhat indifferent to the experience. Since we didn't have a relationship, that deathbed exchange was the first time I'd ever met him. In my twelve-year-old mind, my dad's father simply passed away. I didn't even personalize it as "my grandfather" because that was our only contact with one another. When I returned home, I remember putting the Bible in the bottom drawer of my dresser. I did not pick it back up again until I turned twenty years old.

That's the age at which I was born again. My conversion happened on the heels of college graduation. I was living in a dormitory in New Jersey, which seemed worlds away from my family and childhood home in Queens, New York. I returned home for a short summer break before going on to graduate school. For some reason I needed something from my bottom drawer. As I opened it, the Bible stared me in the face. It now meant the world to me. This was God's love letter to humanity.

It was my road map to every aspect of life and faith. If I was to grow in Christ, this book must become my companion. I slowly opened it. The inscription hit me like a ton of bricks. It read, "To David from Grandfather." As I read and reread it, I could not shake the power of this simple statement. My grandfather, whom I only met on his deathbed, thought enough about me to leave me a priceless legacy: faith in God.

He did not leave me any money. He did not leave me any land. He left me something far more valuable. He left me a spiritual legacy—a way to connect with God.

This is the primary role of a parent and a grandparent. We are to leave a spiritual legacy to our kids. What better legacy than a good prayer life?

If you can leave your children money as an inheritance, leave it. If you can leave them property, by all means do so. But more importantly, gift them with an unconquerable faith, an unstoppable drive, and an insatiable passion to serve Jesus Christ. Give them a God legacy!

A PRAYING PARENT

The apostle Paul had to point out Timothy's spiritual legacy. It was a vital part of who he was. It helped shape him as a man, a Christ-follower, and an emerging apostle. Timothy's actions prompted Paul to write: "I am reminded of your sincere faith, which first lived in your grandmother Lois and in your mother Eunice and, I am persuaded, now lives in you also" (2 Tim. 1:5,

NIV). Young Timothy became the recipient of a trans-generational legacy. Two generations of praying women shaped him from the inside out.

Timothy's home life, created by the faith of his grand-mother and mother, left an indelible mark on him. His grandma and mom were praying women. And their behavior shaped his. The stark reality is you cannot take someone where you've never been yourself. To raise praying children means that you must first have a mea-sure of proficiency yourself. In the book *No Easy Road* Dick Eastman says: "To learn prayer we must pray. We only learn prayer's deepest depths in prayer, not from books. We reach prayer's highest heights in prayer, not from sermons."[1]

Eastman's observation is not isolated. E. M. Bounds, the prolific author of numerous books on prayer, notes: "Prayer is a trade to be learned. We must be appren-tices and serve our time at it. Painstaking care, much thought, practice and labour are required to be a skillful tradesman in praying."[2] Would you attempt to teach your child to swim if you were uncomfortable in the water?

Susanna Wesley, the mother of John and Charles Wesley—founding brothers of the Methodist Church—had nineteen children. Seldom did she miss a daily hour of prayer. Even with the stress and time commitment of mothering, she made time to be with God. She had no private room or dedicated space in which to go and seek the Lord. Yet that didn't stop her. This habit made it easy for her to model prayer to her kids. Eastman documents Susanna's practice like this: "At her chosen time for spiritual exercise she would take her apron and pull it over her face. Her children were instructed never to disturb 'mother' when she was praying in her apron."[3]

The sight of a praying parent leaves a huge impression on the soul of a child. It trumps any verbal instruction that you'll ever give to your little one on prayer. This observation caused leading pastor and author Rick Warren to say: "A dad stands tallest when he kneels to pray with his children."[4]

Susanna Wesley taught each of her children the Lord's Prayer (Matt. 6:9–12) as soon as they could speak. She made them recite it twice daily: when they woke and again at bedtime. As they got older, she added other elements to their prayer regimen. They would be taught to pray for their parents and some of the promises found in the Bible. This was all based on their stage of development and ability to memorize.[5]

Admittedly we're living in a different era with different cultural norms and expectations. But as Christians we should never veer from this parental target: "Train up a child in the way he should go, and when he is old he will not depart from it" (Prov. 22:6). *The Message* puts it this way: "Point your kids in the right direction—when they're old they won't be lost." We cannot cave in to popular culture that suggests that we leave our children to form their own opinions about God, about faith, or about prayer. God demands us to take on the role of a teacher—a teacher of prayer. We come full circle to my point: to raise a child who prays, you must be a "pray-er"!

I saw the truth of this at a conference where the speaker kept me on the edge of my seat as she shared from the Word. Her sermon was on a topic I'd heard a thousand times: *prayer*. As a pastor for some thirty years, I had preached on it at least a hundred times. Yet there was something different in Theresa's preaching. Her knowledge was not simply academic. She was an experienced intercessor.

But that wasn't all. I listened intently, trying to understand why such a basic subject kept hundreds of pastors in rapt attention. We were like clay in her hands. I suspect most of us were seminary-trained. Preaching was our craft, our skill, and our area of proficiency. It's not easy for a preacher to render another preacher spellbound, but Theresa had "it." Halfway through the sermon the source of her anointing became clearer. She said, "As a child I used to wake up sometimes in the middle of the night to go to the bathroom, and I would see my dad in the living room on his knees praying. Sometimes I would hear his loud sobs as he asked God to save his children. He was praying for my soul. He was also praying for the conversion of my seven siblings."

At that she paused, as if she had momentarily left the room, taken captive by her vivid childhood memories of a praying father. It was so moving that I felt like I was carried along with her. It dawned on me; a praying parent is the best foundation for raising a praying child.

In fact, author and teacher Mark Batterson writes: "Prayer turns ordinary parents into prophets who shape the destinies of their children, grandchildren, and every generation that follows."[6] Theresa's life and ministry testified of this fact. You don't have to be a perfect parent, but be a praying parent! God's involvement with the rearing of your child will fill in the parenting gaps that you were unable to perform.

TAKING THE FIRST STEP

Marlinda and I have been married more than thirty years. We have two adult daughters. As you know, parenting is a grueling job. Yet it is a job I wouldn't give up for anything in the world. I love being a dad. I soon discovered that it's easy to love being a dad, but having what it takes to be a *good* dad is quite difficult. To score an A-plus as a parent means that you often have to settle for a C average in other areas. But even though it's extremely hard for us parents to ever earn an A-plus, the mere effort is worth it.

Prayer has to become a real part of your life—every aspect of your life. In other words, you cannot be a praying parent simply for your kids' sake, just as you cannot decide to become born again for their sake. Certainly your children will benefit from your decision to serve Christ. But the decision to serve Christ must first come from the acknowledgment that *you* need Him.

It's just like what flight attendants instruct passengers before the airplane takes off. They say, "Ladies and gentlemen...in the event of a decompression, an oxygen mask will automatically appear in front of you. To start the flow of oxygen, pull the mask toward you. Place it firmly over your nose and mouth....If you are traveling with a child or someone who requires assistance, secure your mask on first, and then assist the other person."[7] In other words, put on your oxygen mask first.

If you want prayer to be an important part of your child's life, you will probably need to reorder the priorities in your own life. It takes time to pray. I am not suggesting that prayer must occupy the bulk of your day. It doesn't have to. Even if you block out fifteen minutes each day for private, focused time with God, you will be making tremendous headway into developing a genuine lifestyle of prayer. Certainly you have fifteen minutes. Each day has ninety-six fifteen-minute blocks. Choose one. Establish a prayer time that is workable and regular. Even if you have to throw an apron over your head as Susanna Wesley did to avoid interruptions, do it. The impact will be tremendous.

TAKE THE SECOND STEP TOO

Prayer is God's invitation into your affairs. Without it you are on your own. Prayerlessness will cause you to function like all the other people in your life, and our world, who don't know God. They fight their own battles. They rely totally on their own wisdom, their own knowledge, and their own resources. Never turning to God for help, they are totally satisfied in the limits of their humanity. You cannot emulate them. They are misguided.

Prayer is a gift that God has given to the human race. It is simply talking to God. God calls for it! He inspires it! He responds to it! Prayer gives you equal access to God, similar to that of angels and archangels. The psalmist says: "Blessed are they who keep his statues and seek him with all their heart" (Ps. 119:2, NIV). Jesus placed top priority on prayer. He taught His disciples that prayer moves God. In other words, there is a cause and effect when you pray. This is the true power of prayer. In Alexander Whyte's classic sermon "The Magnificence of Prayer" he says: "'Why has God established prayer?' asks [French philosopher Blaise] Pascal. His first answer was: 'to communicate to His creatures the dignity of causality.'"[8] Prayer gives us a taste of what it means to move the Almighty. Our prayer *causes* God to respond. When you're convinced of this fact, you are on your way to becoming a praying parent.

Jack, a father of four, put his conviction on the line when his twelve-year-old daughter, Julia, asked for a birthday party he couldn't afford. He could have simply said, "No." But instead he said, "Why don't you pray and ask God for the money you need for this party?" Julia took him up on his offer. Within the next two weeks several hundred dollars flowed into the family's coffers. Every dime was unexpected. They hosted a fabulous party. Julia's prayers paid the bill!

When a parent remains convinced of God's ability and willingness to answer prayer, it makes raising their child to pray all the easier. Paul used the same method when he wrote to the church at Colossae. He asked them to pray for him. Convinced that God would display His power in answer to *their* prayers, Paul said: "Devote yourselves to prayer, being watchful and thankful. And pray for us, too, that God may open a door for our message, so that we may proclaim the mystery of Christ, for which I am in chains" (Col. 4:2–3, NIV).

Paul wanted them to enjoy the same constant attention and active readiness of prayer that he practiced. When you're convinced of the power of prayer, you will be sure to practice watchfulness and thankfulness—two guiding principles of a lifestyle of prayer. In prayer God allows us to see, hear, and notice things that otherwise would be oblivious to our natural mind. This is why a regular prayer time is crucial. Realize that "prayers are prophecies. They are the best predictors of your spiritual future. Who you become is determined by how you pray. Ultimately, the transcript of your prayers becomes the script of your life," as Mark Batterson wrote.[9]

Make sure your prayers are not filled with requests for stuff and more stuff. Express appreciation to God regularly for the many opportunities, blessings, and even the challenges He allows to come your way. A thankful heart is a heart convinced in the power of prayer and the power of God.

In 1892 American-born John Hyde, who later became known as "Praying Hyde," sailed to India to serve as a missionary. In the book *Heroes of the Holy Life* we learn that in one remote village Hyde won a number of men to the Lord, but their wives refused to respond. One morning he awoke with a headache so bad he couldn't get out of bed. Because his custom was to thank God for everything, he thanked God for his headache. His desire to win souls to Jesus caused him to ask to be carried on his bed and placed under a shade tree by the side of the road. When the village women learned how ill he was, one by one they came to his bedside to sympathize, and he used their visits as an opportunity to witness. That day he led many to the Lord, and that night had a baptism service where several were water baptized.[10]

What would happen if you practiced *thankfulness*? Expressing thanks to God regularly would shape your prayer life and the other dimensions of your life in untold ways. Not only would you benefit from having a healthier perspective and a happier home, but you would also have a better emotional disposition. Your kids, spouse, and perhaps even the family pet would like hanging around you more. Your treatment of them would improve because your interior life improved.

When Paul invited the Colossians to pray for him, it was not simply an affirmation of his conviction of the value and power of prayer; it was an opportunity for them to develop that same perspective toward prayer.

He was their spiritual father, and he needed to parent them in this area of their spiritual development.

THE RESPONSIBILITY OF A PRAYING PARENT

No one can guide your child's spiritual growth but you. Today there is a lucrative industry centered on the outsourcing of parental duties. For example, a five-day sleep training plan for infants costs around $350. One agency charges parents $1,250 to child-proof their home with expert latching, gating, and locking, as well as lead-testing. This service includes CPR and car seat training. The more difficult jobs cost more; getting your kid to stop thumb sucking in two sessions will cost you a whopping $4,300. Potty training in two weeks with a live-in instructor would cost a mere $3,700. Teaching your child to say "please" and "thank you" and how to behave in public, shake hands, talk on the phone, and hold a fork is only $85.

This may sound funny, but the point is that too many busy, dual-career parents try to cut corners by writing a check to cover parental responsibilities. I'm surprised that I didn't find prayer training included in any of the outsourcing packages. Perhaps the reason I didn't find it there is because many parents expect the church to assume total responsibility for the spiritual development of their children. That is not the church's job! The church supplements, but doesn't replace, home training. It comes alongside of parents to reinforce and undergird their efforts, but they must take the lead in the spiritual development of their child's prayer life.

After all, your influence over your child will be greater than that of any church, no matter how great its training. Your child is with you most of the time. They're typically only at church for ninety minutes once a week, and that hour and a half is shrinking, because church attendance is on the decline.[11]

Children are precious gifts God has entrusted to us until adulthood. It is our responsibility to help them develop into mature adults who have great power on bended knees. As a pastor I am brutally aware that your words, as a parent, will mean more to your kids than mine will ever mean. Especially in their formative years they cling to your words. You cannot hold to an ecclesiastical framework that pins the work of parenting on the shoulders of spiritual leaders or the organized church. They are your kids! The final responsibility is yours!

In his book *The Forgotten Ways* Alan Hirsch writes: "Take the Chinese [underground church]...when most of their leaders and theologians [have been] killed or imprisoned and all access to outside sources is cut off, they are somehow forced through sheer circumstances to unlock something truly potent and compelling in the message they carry as the people of God."[12] What Dr. Hirsch is pointing out is that the Chinese Christians were forced to take responsibility for their spiritual formation instead of placing it on the shoulders of the organized church. The ordained clergy could not assume the sole responsibility of being "the keepers of God's spiritual secrets." The entire church had to know how to pray and train one another in the art of prayer. Consequently the underground church in China numbers in the millions. And it is quite strong in prayer and other disciplines.

Pretend that, as a parent, you are the underground church. My role, as a pastor, is to empower you—the parent. I need your help to help you. If you accept that you are the principal prayer-trainer for your child, we will see an organic multiplication of praying parents who raise up praying children.

I don't mind that your empowerment would lead to a decentralized church. This is what we need if we are going to impact the world for Jesus Christ. The more prayer-empowered parents there are, the more prayer-empowered kids we'll have.

KEEP PRESSING ON

Becoming a praying parent will take time. There will be lots of starts and stops. But keep pressing on. Even if you've not been a perfect role model of a praying parent, you cannot allow your past to sabotage your future. We Christians are comeback people.

Former *CBS Evening News* anchor Dan Rather, who boxed in high school, says his coach's greatest goal was to teach his boxers that they absolutely, positively, without question, had to be "get up" fighters.

In boxing you're on your own; there's no place to hide....At the end of the match only one boxer has his hands up. That's it. He has no one to credit or to blame except himself.

If you're in a ring just once in your life—completely on your own—and you get knocked down but you get back up again, it's a never-to-be-forgotten experience. Your sense of achievement is distinct and unique. And sometimes the only thing making you get up is someone in your corner yelling.[13]

We Christians are "get up" fighters. Scripture declares: "For though the righteous fall seven times, they rise again" (Prov. 24:16, NIV). Repentance is God's way of helping us to get back up on our feet. Having seen your neglect of prayer, don't stay knocked down on the ground disgusted at yourself. Get up! Repent and rise! Become a praying parent! This is God's call upon your life.

ACTION STEPS

Thank God for His grace. This empowering presence of God—that's what grace is—enables you to be what He's called you to be and do what He's called you to do. Because of God's amazing grace, declare, "I can":

- Become a powerful praying parent.

- Develop the habits of an intercessor. By first becoming a praying parent, I will be able to help my child become a praying child.

- Repent of my old prayer habits.

Now, find a quiet space to offer this prayer:

Gracious God, thank You for Your amazing forgiveness. Forgive me for not being diligent in creating great prayer habits. I want to start over. May today become the first day of my new prayer lifestyle! Help me to spend quality time with You daily. I ask You this in the name of Jesus. Amen.

Chapter 2

THE POWER OF A
PRAYING CHILD

———— ✹ ————

A YOUNG BOY'S DAD always closed grace at supper time with these words, "Come, Lord Jesus, be our guest and bless what You have provided."

One evening the little boy couldn't hold back his gnawing question regarding his dad's unusual prayer. So he asked, "Dad, why do you ask Jesus to come and be our guest, but He never comes?"

His dad lovingly said, "Son, we can only wait. The Lord will not ignore our invitation. One day He'll come. And we must be ready."

The boy then gave a follow-up question, "If we expect Jesus to join us for dinner, how come we don't set a place for Him at the table?" Realizing his son had a point, the dad permitted his little guy to put another place setting at the table. Almost instantaneously there was a faint knock on the door. When they opened it, to their surprise there stood a shivering little boy with barely enough clothes to cover his body. They quickly invited him in and immediately threw a blanket around him to warm his freezing little body.

Suddenly it all made sense to the son. He turned to his dad and said, "I guess Jesus couldn't come today, so he sent this poor little boy instead." Without any delay they offered the little visitor a place at the dinner table.[1]

I love kids. They are so innocent and trusting. What we call "faith," they call "normal." This is why it's so great to talk to them about prayer when they are young and receptive.

The innocence of the son in the opening story is so touching. His perspective gives us a glimpse as to how kids approach prayer. They can talk to God about anything—even the things we adults would never dare say.

A five-year-old said grace at family dinner one night: "Dear God, thank You for these pancakes." When he finished, his parents asked him why he thanked God for pancakes when they were having chicken. He smiled and said, "I thought I'd see if He was paying attention tonight."

Other times when kids pray, it's not comedic. It's rather serious. Their little hearts are bothered by something, or their minds long for something special. This was the case with four-year-old Michelle, as her mother shared in a story in *Guideposts*.

One night as the mother was tucking her four-year-old daughter Michelle into bed, she allowed space for Michelle to pray what was on her heart. Michelle, in her innocent, childlike manner simply asked God, "Please let me see a frog tonight, in Jesus's name. Amen."

The mother thought Michelle's prayer was cute, but that it wouldn't be answered. She didn't dare tell her that. She simply said, "I haven't seen any frogs this year; we'll just have to wait and see." Without any hesitating Michelle blurted out, "God can do anything. Just like Daddy."

Michelle was undaunted. She trusted in her earthly dad and her heavenly Father. Her mother, on the other hand, struggled to hang on to her once stalwart faith. As she walked out of Michelle's room, she prayed "God...do You hear her? Do You hear me?"

The mother went to the garage to move the load of clothes that she had in the washing machine. As she turned on the lights in the garage and started to place the wet clothes into the dryer, she heard a little commotion near the garage door. Their dog also heard the noise and ran toward the sound, barking as he went.

He stood there yapping away at what he saw. When she drew close, she saw a frog in the corner of the garage. She ran to Michelle's room, waking her up.

"Michelle, wake up. Look," she said. "God really answered your prayer." Michelle stared at her while wiping the sleepiness from her eyes. She picked him up, petted him, and then said, "I knew He would." That was it. No fanfare. No loud shouts of excitement. She just matter-of-factly gave her response to seeing a frog—the answer to her prayers—and then went back to sleep.

Michelle's mother knew the answer to her daughter's prayer was also God's answer to her cry for a renewed faith.[2]

Michelle's request might have sounded strange to her mom, but God, her loving Father, wanted to answer her. And He did. How do you raise your children to have that same kind of power when they pray?

There were three guiding principles at work in Daniel's life as a young boy. As a captive of war Daniel was brought against his will into Babylon. This Israelite boy, a foreigner in a new land, quickly distinguished himself among the other young men inducted into the Royal Academy (Dan. 1:4–17). One principal reason was that he knew the power of prayer and continued in that lifestyle throughout his youth and adulthood. Your children can do the same. From Daniel's life we conclude that:

- Children must know the purpose of prayer.

- Children must establish a pattern of prayer.

- Children must develop power in prayer.

Children Must Know the Purpose of Prayer

Everyone has a purpose. You are not an accident. Similarly *everything* has a purpose. This extends to spiritual activities, including prayer. Knowing something's purpose allows you to give yourself over to it without inhibition.

Prayer allows you to talk with God.

When you pray, you connect with God. Jesus modeled this throughout His earthly ministry. He often pulled away from the crowd to be alone with God. In fact, we read: "Very early in the morning, while it was still dark, Jesus got up, left the house and went off to a solitary place, where he prayed" (Mark 1:35, NIV). Prayer positions you Godward. It forces you to scrutinize your motives, desires, and attitudes. Apart from asking God for help, the sacredness of praying increases your likelihood of making sound decisions.

The director of our children's church asked five-year-old Emma to pray. She said, "I don't know how to."

He said, "Just talk to God like you would to a friend or an ordinary person."

Closing her eyes, Emma prayed: "Hi, God! How's it going? OK; bye, God." Her innocence was cute. But it captured the meaning of prayer—talking to God.

Prayer gives you strength.

Prayer allows you to tap into God's strength. It also provides a forum for you to request something from Him. Jesus taught that you should "ask and it will be given to you; seek and you will find; knock and the door will be opened to you. For everyone who asks receives; the one who seeks finds; and to the one who knocks, the door will be opened" (Luke 11:9–10, NIV). This verse provides a focused understanding of a dimension of prayer. We are free to ask God for His help. When you feel weak, discouraged, or beaten down, prayer gives you strength.

Do you remember the famous story of Daniel in the lions' den? Daniel was an adult at the time. As a foreigner he had risen to a very prestigious government job as one of three administrators overseeing the entire country of Babylon. Daniel's leadership ability was so good the king was set to promote him over his two colleagues, and they were not too happy about it (Dan. 6:3–4). Out of jealousy they pressured King Darius to establish an irrevocable law that punished its violators by having them thrown into a lions' den. Anyone found praying to anyone other than the king over a thirty-day period would suffer this tragedy (Dan. 6:6–7).

Daniel prayed to God for strength to deal with this oppressive law (Dan. 6:11). Eventually he was thrown into the lions' den, but he survived a nightlong stint. The lions didn't harm him. Through this and other miraculous experiences Daniel knew the purpose of prayer. Prayer is talking to God about anything that you're facing.

CHILDREN MUST ESTABLISH
A PATTERN OF PRAYER

Good habits come from good training or the adoption of good patterns. Good patterns provide focus and strategy to achieve your goals. The champion boxer Muhammad Ali said: "I hated every minute of training, but I said, 'Don't quit. Suffer now and live the rest of your life as a champion.'"[3] To master the habit of prayer, children need to develop patterns.

Set a place of prayer.

The moment Daniel became privy to King Darius's decree, "he went home to *his upstairs room* where the windows opened toward Jerusalem. Three times a day he got down on his knees and prayed, giving thanks to his God, just as he had done before" (Dan. 6:10, NIV, emphasis added). Daniel had an established place where he prayed. God is omnipresent. He is everywhere at once. But to help your child develop power in prayer, you must instill this habit.

Daniel developed the habit of praying in a set place. This is a useful tip because children thrive on predictability. While teaching on prayer, Jesus said: "But when you pray, *go into your room*, close the door and pray to your Father" (Matt. 6:6, NIV, emphasis added). This suggests that we ought to have a set place to pray. It is the same pattern Daniel had established.

Heartfelt prayer is best done in a private space with limited distractions. If you don't have that luxury, take a page out of the playbook of Susanna Wesley, who threw her apron over her head and spent an hour in prayer daily. The apron provided her with a measure of privacy from the moving about of her nineteen children. There are times my wife and I are sitting down in our living room and Marlinda will say: "I'm going upstairs to pray." I do the same thing. As empty nesters we have a couple of extra bedrooms that we use as private prayer spaces.

Your regular prayer place could be a bathroom, a kitchen, or even a corner of a bedroom. Several years ago I was in ministry with a popular Christian singer. She said as a child she shared a bedroom with her sister. This did not give her all of the privacy she desired, especially when it came to prayer, so she asked her father if he could turn a portion of her closet into a prayer room. They had dual closets in the bedroom. The dad, moved by his little girl's desire to draw closer to the Lord, went straight to work in renovating her closet. You don't need a lot of space. You just need a familiar space.

An anonymous person wrote:

> My parents were ardent practitioners of prayer. As a child, I was greatly impressed by their daily devotions. Eventually I was such a convert that I thought anything that went wrong could be readily remedied, or anything that I desired could be obtained, if Mother prayed about it.
>
> As I grew older, the nature of my problems and concerns changed and, whenever I voiced doubt or fear, Mother would say, "We had better pray about this." Our secret place was an old hallstand near the front door of our country home. This antique, straight and tall, faced with glass, with clusters of hooks on each side for coats, and a receptacle

near the right-hand side for umbrellas, also had a chest across the bottom which made it convenient and comfortable to rest the elbows while kneeling. This was our favorite altar. To me, it was a place of miracles.[4]

Setting a place of prayer is important because it will not distract your children when they go there daily to connect with God. Your children will learn to treasure their prayer closet much like they treasure their bedroom or their desk.

Set a time of prayer.

Equally important to setting a place for prayer is setting a specific time to pray. Let's go back to the scriptures to understand a different, yet necessary, prayer pattern.

> Now when Daniel learned that the decree had been published, he went home to his upstairs room where the windows opened toward Jerusalem. *Three times a day* he got down on his knees and prayed, giving thanks to his God, just as he had done before.
> —DANIEL 6:10, NIV, EMPHASIS ADDED

Daniel grew as a man of prayer not by simply having a heart after God; he developed regular and consistent prayer times. Think about it. If your kid takes music lessons, she cannot improve unless she practices regularly. The same holds true if she's to improve at ballet, volleyball, or any other activity. The

University of Chicago analyzed the careers of con-
cert pianists, artists, and athletes to determine what
process led to success. The research revealed that the
musicians worked an average of 17.1 years from the day
they began taking piano lessons to the day they won a
major competition.[5]

Children must give the same level of discipline to
prayer. Your vision for your child to have power on
bended knees is fabulous. To achieve it, however, calls
for him to develop habits and personal disciplines that
begin with an appeal to be a better kid. Help him see
that he's called to be an awesome disciple of Jesus even
while he's a kid. Similar to Moses, your child is no *ordinary child* (Acts 7:20). None of our children are. They
are God's children—King's kids.

Help your child to set a daily time of prayer just as you
help them to know when to brush their teeth or practice their piano drills. You have to remind them until it
becomes a habit. Teach them to set a prayer time and to
guard it. In chapter 1 I encouraged you to start a prayer
time that was doable—fifteen minutes a day until you
can do more. Do the same with your child. Remember
that doable for a little one may be five minutes. Start off
with one minute and then build to five over time. The
power of prayer is not the length of prayer. It's the sincerity of the heart and the authentic connection one has
with God. Let that be your focus!

Set an agenda of prayer.

Your child is going to want to know: "What should I pray about?" Once again we can draw our answer from Daniel's story of the lions' den. I want to keep that scripture in front of you so that you see its value. I'll emphasize a different part of the passage this time.

> Now when Daniel learned that the decree had been published, he went home to his upstairs room where *the windows opened toward Jerusalem.* Three times a day he got down on his knees and prayed giving thanks to God, just as he had done before.
> —DANIEL 6:10, NIV, EMPHASIS ADDED

Apart from the present problem of his being tossed into a lions' den, the text gives us a glimpse of Daniel's regular prayer agenda. Being a Jewish immigrant living away from his people and his homeland, his heart longed for Jerusalem. Daniel focused his prayer agenda on the welfare of his people back home. He kept the topic of Jerusalem on his prayer list. Your children can be taught to pray for the people on their heart—their family members, school friends, neighbors, and others.

Daniel physically positioned himself toward Jerusalem. He couldn't see this distant city from the window of his prayer room, but the direction captured his view. It helped him to form a mental picture of the city and God's promises. Teach your children that they can cut out a picture of something that helps them visualize one of God's unmet promises for their life or a need in the family. A picture of something they are passionate about can also help them find the right words to use in prayer.

Perhaps you can help them develop a prayer board—like a vision board. It could be as simple as a poster board with cutouts representing things your child longs to see God do for them. This activity will bring you two closer and also help your children see prayer as something practical. Their prayers can also be basically their thanking God for His blessings. Maybe on the prayer board you can paste a picture of grandma, who is in need of God's healing.

Children Must Develop Power in Prayer

Power speaks of strength, confidence, and trust in God's ability. The apostle John says: "This is the confidence that we have in Him, that if we ask anything according to His will, He hears us. So if we know that He hears whatever we ask, we know that we have whatever we asked of Him" (1 John 5:14–15). We all want to have confidence that our prayers matter to God. Knowing that He hears and answers us is the crux of the matter. Kids will only pray when they have this assurance. Without it their prayer closet will remain empty. There are five habits I regularly practice to grow in confidence towards God. I shared them with my daughters. I'm passing them on to you in the hopes that you will pass them on to your children.

I read great books on prayer.

Books on prayer capture personal accounts of other Christ-followers who sought to build a life of prayer. Their testimonies provide encouragement, insights into the nature of God, and confirmation that God is the same yesterday, today, and forever. Here are three books on prayer that you can read to your kids:

- *I Can Pray!* by Suzette T. Caldwell (for ages three to seven)

- *What Happens When I Talk to God? The Power of Prayer for Boys and Girls* by Stormie Omartian (for ages three to seven)

- *Peter's Perfect Prayer Place* by Stephen and Alex Kendrick (for ages four to eight)

When I read *Hudson Taylor's Spiritual Secrets*, I learned that—as a young man in England—this great missionary to China came to the realization: "When I get to China…I shall have no claim on anyone for anything. My only claim will be on God. How important to learn, before leaving England, to move man, through God, by prayer alone. My kind employer wished me to remind him whenever my salary became due. This I determined not to do directly, but to ask that God would bring the fact to his recollection, and thus encourage me by answering prayer."[6]

I would not have learned this little confidence-building truth apart from the insights found in that book.

I listen to great sermons on prayer.

The Internet gives us access to an enormous treasure trove of sermons. You have the ability to hear historic giants, such as Billy Graham, Mother Teresa, Archbishop Desmond Tutu, and Dr. Martin Luther King Jr., and leading scholars and thinkers such as Dr. John R. W. Stott expound on the power of prayer.

Some organizations have even taken to having artists dramatize some of the historic sermons preached by the nineteenth-century preacher Charles Haddon Spurgeon. I have grown immensely from listening to his sermons on prayer. You can do the same through his sermons and those of other great preachers. This will equip you to pass on timeless truths to your children. If your child doesn't have the attention span to listen to a full-length sermon, consider breaking it up in five-minute increments. Discuss each segment with him so that he'll learn through the conversation.

I study the lives of great intercessors.

In order to have an impact on your child's prayer life, consider watching the movie *War Room* together. It is family-friendly and helps children and adults alike to have an appetite for prayer. Nine-year-old Jonathan was so moved after watching *War Room* with his parents that he moved all of his clothes to one side of his closet and placed a stool in the empty part. Like it was depicted in the movie, he turned his closet into a prayer room—a war room—where he could have a set place to seek the Lord. Jonathan would sit on the stool as he daily communed with God.

As an adult you can gain nuggets from studying the lives of historic intercessors. Have you ever heard of Daniel Nash? I'm sure you'll know the name of the man he served in tireless intercession. Nash was the primary intercessor for Charles G. Finney—an eighteenth-century evangelist famous for leading hundreds of thousands into a relationship with Christ. Finney's forte was revival—the awakening of spiritual sight to lost people and the reawakening of spiritual intimacy to existing Christians. Finney credits much of his success to the prayer ministry of Father Nash, as Finney affectionately called him.

God used Finney to travel along the eastern seaboard of the United States, as well as to England a few times. On a recent speaking engagement in Rochester, New York—a place where revival broke out in the 1800s under the ministry of Charles Finney—my friend and senior pastor of The Father's House, Pierre DuPlessis, showed me a picture of the tombstone of Daniel Nash. In addition to noting his name and the years marking his life's span, the headstone read: "Laborer with Finney. Mighty in Prayer." Nash would often go to a town a few weeks ahead of Finney and check himself into a room. He'd then spend weeks in fasting and prayer for a mighty move of God to occur in that city. When Finney arrived to preach, the results were phenomenal. Father Nash's prayers paved the way for the preaching.

Another intercessor that I have come to admire is John Hyde, the missionary to India I mentioned in chapter 1. The aforementioned book *Heroes of the Holy Life* describes how his first few years there were difficult because he struggled to learn the language. The missionary organization voted to send him back to the States. The Indian people protested, saying, "If he never speaks the language of our lips, he speaks the language of our hearts."[7]

Hyde's prayer life created such a big heart toward the Indian people that it was unmistakable even though he struggled in picking up their language. From this historic intercessor I learned how a lifestyle of prayer can make up for your shortcomings.

I spend great times in prayer.

It's wonderful to read great books on prayer, listen to great sermons on prayer, and even to study the lives of great intercessors, but nothing can replace your own time on bended knees. I have spent great times in prayer as I write this book. I've spent time praying for you, although we may never meet. I have spent great times praying for your children—the intended recipient of the advice of this book. I'm convinced that if God doesn't open your heart to the power of prayer and that of your children, this book and all the others you may come across will be of little use.

The celebrated preacher J. H. Jowett said: "It is in the field of prayer that life's critical battles are lost or won.

We must conquer all our circumstances there. We must first of all bring them there. We must survey them there. We must master them there. In prayer we bring our spiritual enemies into the Presence of God and we fight them there. Have you tried that? Or have you been satisfied to meet and fight your foes in the open spaces of the world?"[8] The practice of prayer is a learned one. You cannot avoid your personal moments in the presence of God. Neither can your children. This is where power is established.

I share my great answers to prayer.

Our God is not just a prayer-hearing God: He's a prayer-answering God. I am pumped when God answers my prayers. I can't help but broadcast them with my family and beyond. I've prayed for children to be impacted in a unique way through my writing ministry. Seeing this book go far and wide is an answer to prayer. Hearing of its impact upon your child via your prayer training will be another great answer to prayer.

Years ago I used to have a radio program called *IMPACT with Dr. David Ireland*. When it first became an idea, I found myself praying for an announcer. The program couldn't become a reality without an announcer. I envisioned a man with a deep resonant voice that just commands attention. One evening, as I was praying at my desk, there was a knock on my office door. When I opened it, there stood Greg Thompson, a member of my congregation whom I vaguely knew.

He had tears rolling down his cheeks. Let me help you visualize what I saw: there in front of me stood a medium-built, African American man about forty years old, six feet tall, and meticulously dressed, with a handsome, bearded face.

Surprised to see him outside of a Sunday morning and standing in front of my office crying, I quickly welcomed him in. His tears told me that this was no time for social niceties. I got right to it. I asked, "What's wrong?" Amidst sobs he was able to say that he couldn't shake it. "Shake what?" I asked.

Greg said, "Can you use me? Can you use me? I used to be a radio DJ in college. I just need to use my talent." While he was speaking, his rich baritone voice made his tearful words sound so Shakespearean. He sounded almost like James Earl Jones—you likely know the actor who does the Verizon commercials and is also heard saying, "This is CNN."

I smiled. This was an answer to prayer—a great answer to prayer. It was an answer to prayer for both of us. When I shared with Greg that I had been praying about the need for a radio announcer, he laughed. I laughed too. God is amazing. Again I came to that conclusion. Answered prayer brought me there. It will do the same for you and your children.

Be patient with your children as you help them learn how to wield the power of a praying child. It takes time to master the discipline and practice of prayer. You know that. Give them time to discover the same.

ACTION STEPS

There are some things you can do today to get started in the training process of your children in the art of prayer. Here are a few coaching tips and reminders:

- The story about Daniel in the lions' den captures rich lessons on how to teach children to pray.

- The power of a praying child is unleashed as children know the purpose of prayer, establish a pattern of prayer, and develop power in prayer.

Take some time to scout out a good space for your child to pray. Offer him a few options and together decide what would work best. Perhaps you can prayer together for the first time in that space. Might I suggest this prayer to start your special moment with God:

> *Dear Lord, I love spending special moments with You. May I always come here to seek Your face and to hear Your heart when I'm troubled and confused. May I always find peace and strength in Your presence. This I pray in the mighty name of Jesus. Amen.*

It's your turn now. Pray.

Chapter 3

JESUS–THE FIRST TWELVE YEARS

———— ☼ ————

T HE SOUND OF her little voice was heard praying over the video monitor. After tucking in their two-year-old daughter for the night, Caleb and Kathryn Whitt had forgotten to pray with her. Sutton did not forget, however. She laid in her crib for an hour, thanking God for each person in her life. She went right down the list, personalizing her prayers. At times Sutton repeated the names on her mental prayer list. When she finished praying, "Thank You, God, for Mommy," "Thank You, God, for Daddy," and other various requests, the praying toddler said, "Amen," and then drifted off to sleep. The proud parents posted the video on their Facebook page, and as of this writing they've received more than 168,000 views. *Good Morning America* even featured a story on this praying toddler.[1] If little two-year-old Sutton prays, your child can too.

God's heart for children is without dispute. I love the way *The Message* version of Psalm 127:3–4 lays out God's feelings about kids. Solomon writes:

> Don't you see that children are God's best gift?
> the fruit of the womb his generous legacy? Like
> a warrior's fistful of arrows are the children of a
> vigorous youth.

The song captured Israel's heart and made it into God's eternal song book—the Bible. The message is timeless. Children are God's best gift. This truth is unquestioned. To demonstrate our gratitude to God, we must teach our children how to have a genuine relationship with Him. Healthy relationships are built on communication. Prayer simply means communicating with God. In fact, prayer is the cornerstone of a healthy relationship with God.

Throughout the Bible we have examples of children with strong relationships with God, from Samuel, Uzziah, and Josiah in the Old Testament to John the Baptist and Jesus in the New Testament. None of these young intercessors prayed simply to please their parents. It may have started off as an act of obedience, but it could never continue that way. Intercessors are not forced to pray. Intercession is an act of love. When you pray, you're speaking God's love language. Intercessors, young and old alike, pray because their hearts are gripped by the reality of a loving God. As the Bible depicts, parents play a crucial role in the formative years of young intercessors. Let's explore the prayer life of Jesus when He was a child.

JESUS–THE EARLY YEARS

Before there was a cross, there was a cradle. Jesus did not skip steps on the way to the cross. He had to progress through all of the ordinary, yet necessary, stages of human development. Scholars use the terms *very God* and *very man* to describe the unique nature of Jesus. He was totally God while at the same time totally man. His humanity did not take away from His divinity. His divinity did not suppress or deny His humanity. In fact, being human enabled Jesus to sympathize with our weaknesses, as our High Priest (Heb. 4:15). He accurately and compassionately brings our suffering before God's throne of grace.

Jesus's prayer life had a starting point, just like yours, mine, and our children's. Jesus was a baby, a preteen, a teenager, and a young adult before He made His mark on the world as an adult. The Bible gives us little bits and pieces of His life prior to adulthood. We have enough to form this conclusion: God does not wait until you're an adult to respond to your prayers.

Jesus, the praying child

At the age of twelve Jesus understood the importance and value of prayer. He participated in prayer— His Father's business—and other spiritual matters. Jesus made that point very clear to His earthly parents.

Unbeknownst to Mary and Joseph, on their return trip home from the annual Feast of the Passover, Jesus stayed behind. Like all parents, when they realized He was not in the caravan with any of the other families, they returned to Jerusalem in search of their little boy. When they found Him, Jesus respectfully said: "Why were you searching for me?...Didn't you know I had to be in my Father's house?" (Luke 2:49, NIV).

What did Jesus mean by this? What was this twelve-year-old doing? The answer is found when we understand what occurs in the temple. Years later, as an adult, Jesus said: "My house shall be called a *house of prayer* for all nations" (Mark 11:17, emphasis added). Jesus used the terms "My house" and "My Father's house" (John 2:16) interchangeably. Both terms reference the temple as a place of prayer, among other religious activities. Without reading anything into the text, we can easily see that Jesus prayed as a child.

If the Father valued, respected, and answered Jesus's prayers while a child, God also values the prayers of your children.

The influence of Mary and Joseph

As parents Mary and Joseph created a certain home environment, family culture, and expectation about Jesus. Even if their influence on Him was limited, flawed, or partial, they still played a role in His spiritual development. Joseph was a carpenter (Matt. 13:55). Jesus became a carpenter (Mark 6:3). Jewish boys, in those days, went into the same line of business as their father. Becoming a carpenter was no accident. We know that parental influence was at work in Jesus's life. It didn't stop at His vocational choice. It extended into the whole of His life.

The religious practices of Mary and Joseph are without question. When Jesus was eight days old, like any good Jewish parents, they had Him named and circumcised (Luke 2:21). At the appropriate time they traveled to Jerusalem to dedicate Him to God, in accordance with the Law of Moses (Luke 2:22). Every year Mary and Joseph faithfully went to Jerusalem to celebrate the Feast of the Passover (Luke 2:41). It was during one of these annual visits that Jesus, at twelve years old, remained behind to pray and attend to His "Father's house."

The Bible doesn't detail all the things Jesus learned from the godliness of His parents. Even in their limited knowledge, imperfect lifestyle, and inadequacies in raising the Savior, they still played a critical part. Your role in the spiritual development of your child is invaluable. You cannot deflect it back to God. You cannot claim that your inadequacies disqualify you. Even if they do, you still cannot abdicate your role as an influencer. You can't even say: "*My* parents didn't teach me how to pray. Therefore, I lack the tools to teach my child." None of these excuses hold water even if they are true.

PARENT EVEN WHEN YOU
DON'T UNDERSTAND

Imagine what Mary and Joseph would answer if we asked: "How do you raise a Savior? What do you say to the Son of God when He's troubled about His life's path, purpose, or direction?" Assuming they'd be brutally honest with you, you would probably hear a lot of silence on their part, and understandably so. I know that I couldn't effectively parent the Savior of the world. I had trouble parenting my two little girls, who were as equally flawed and imperfect as their mother and me. What can we learn from Mary and Joseph? One lesson I believe is this: they knew when to be silent and simply treasure things in their hearts.

After the little setback surrounding Jesus's delay at the temple when He was twelve and His reasoned response to His parents, Scripture says:

> Then He [Jesus] went down with them [Mary and Joseph] and came to Nazareth and was obedient to them. But His mother kept all these words in her heart. And Jesus increased in wisdom and in stature, and in favor with God and men.
> —LUKE 2:51–52

Mary did not understand how to fully parent Jesus, but she did know enough to simply keep things in her heart. In other words, she deposited things into the treasure chest of her soul. You must do the same even though your child is not God incarnate. There are aspects of your child, as was the case with mine, in which you will have limited knowledge. You won't know what to do or what to say in every instance. During those times your silence will prove an excellent parental technique. Your silence actually gives space for your child to discover their path and their unique personality. This is a significant part of human development and an important part of parenting.

Most people are familiar with the phrase *helicopter parent*. It describes a parental style that hovers over a child. The kid has no independence or freedom without an obsessive parental eye watching and indulging her. This style of parenting will result in your child becoming a sneaky child, a parent-pleaser, or a dysfunctional adult who is unable to function with a modicum of psychological or emotional maturity. Jesus's spiritual formation included the necessary parental detachment when His actions caused Mary and Joseph to just treasure things in their hearts. Perplexed by His words or His actions, their silence gave Him the necessary freedom to grow in favor with God and men. I encourage you to take a play out of their playbook in the shaping of your home environment.

Your home is the number one influence in the life of your child. The average church has a child 1 percent of his time and the school for 16 percent, but the home for 83 percent of his time. This reality does not eliminate or reduce the need for churches or Christian schools to serve as positive spiritual training centers for your child, but it establishes the fact that your home dominates your child's world and you have an opportunity to maximize that benefit. You must take your role seriously! And if this book has come into your hands after you've raised your kids or made tons of mistakes in their spiritual development, you can still pray for God's goodness to intervene and readjust their life's trajectory.

In a recent speaking engagement in Benin City, Nigeria, I heard the most stirring story from one of the Nigerian speakers. Let's call her Nancy for the sake of anonymity. Nancy poured out her heart to us as she described her journey to faith. Her father was a witch doctor. As Nancy grew up, he never communicated his love to her or her siblings. He was a polygamist with more than twenty children from multiple wives, and his marital status and the habits of polygamy compounded his negative influence on them.

Ironically, although her father was a witch doctor, he was generous toward the local Catholic church. He would donate his services as a contractor to construct or repair portions of the church building. He even attended their services periodically. I know it sounds a bit preposterous to be immersed in witchcraft while frequenting church. Satan is so deceptive that he can twist people's minds and bend their thinking into such a confused state that they don't know how to distinguish right from wrong, black from white, or up from down. This is what happened to Nancy's dad throughout her childhood. She hated it and him.

In the providence of God Nancy became born again. She enrolled in a Bible college in America and returned to Nigeria after graduation. Nancy was an ordained clergy who was still struggling with hate toward her dad, but God finally brought her ugly attitude to an end. The Lord challenged Nancy to have compassion for her misguided father. It wasn't easy, but she did it. She asked God to truly forgive her. The evidence of her repentance surfaced when she was asked to eulogize a friend of the family. Unbeknownst to Nancy, the family friend was also a witch doctor.

Her dad was present at the eulogy, as were his friends, who were also witch doctors. She knew nothing of their involvement in the occult—only her father's. During the eulogy Nancy happened to mention a childhood memory of her father's generosity toward the church. Her few words of love pierced his darkened heart. Little did she know that when she closed out the sermon and gave the invitation for people to make a decision to serve Christ, her dad would be among that group who said yes.

Nancy's story reminds me that no one is too far from the grace of God. Even if your parents did not model exemplary spiritual habits as Jesus's parents did, there is still hope. And if your parents lived in the darkest part of hell, like Nancy's father, God's mercy is still potent enough to rescue you. And with Nancy, God's incredible kindness resulted not only in her conversion but also that of her dad. Now he is a positive influence on his grandkids. The noble place in which he now stands is because of Nancy's bigheartedness. She forgave him. And he learned to forgive himself. You must follow suit, whether you are the one needing forgiveness or the forgiver.

TAKING THE FIRST STEP

Do you see it? The first step in becoming a positive influence in the spiritual life and development of your child is in admitting your imperfection as a parent. My wife, Marlinda, and I sat across the dinner table from this young couple in our church. They are parents of two young children, both under the age of ten. A few minutes into our conversation Michele started crying. It was one of those silent cries. Tears rolled down her cheeks, but there was no noise. We waited patiently, silently, for her to tell us why she was crying. In a few moments Michele stammered: "I feel like such a bad mother." The husband tried to console her, rubbing her back, silently but reassuringly. I understood his actions. So did Marlinda. As seasoned parents—at least that is how we appeared to them, having raised our children—the next words out of our mouths would mean the world to them.

I spoke first. I reassured Michele that the fact she was so broken up about not being the mom she envisioned probably proved just the opposite: she was a good mom! Her husband immediately chimed in, "You're a great mom, sweetheart. Our kids know that, and so do I." As Michele continued wiping the tears from her eyes, Marlinda spoke up, saying, "I know how you feel. I used to struggle with the same feelings when our daughters were little kids. You never think you're doing enough. You always think that you're falling short of the standard. I think we mothers set up an unreachable goal that keeps us in a vicious cycle of self-loathing and depression." Michele's head bobbed up and down, affirming that's how she'd been feeling.

We spent some more time reaffirming them and reminding them that parenting is a marathon, not a sixty-yard dash. But effective parenting begins when you realize that your kids are not looking for perfect parents. They are looking for loving parents.

The spiritual formation of your children starts with your loving them. You cannot score an A-plus in every area of life or every stage in the parental process all the time. But you can love your kids throughout every stage of their development, even during some of their unpleasant moments. Before you can effectively love your kids, though, you have to love yourself. This is also the starting point! If you think the worst about yourself, how will you teach or demonstrate to your kids that God has good things in store for them? Prayer starts with the premise: God loves me and wants my best. Prayer will become a difficult task if the foundation of love is removed from our minds. That is why you have to learn to love yourself. Our parenting springs from this self-love. The effective parent teaches his child to love himself and behave accordingly. Most of this is non-verbal. It's modeled.

Jesus was loved by His parents

Jesus's home life was a nurturing environment. Mary and Joseph loved Him. They also loved each other. Joseph took Mary to be his bride knowing she was pregnant—albeit by the Holy Spirit (Matt. 1:20). For him to wed Mary took a lot of courage and love. It tells us a lot about his character. Joseph even moved his young family out of the country to protect them from Herod's death sentence levied against Jewish boys born during the time of Jesus's birth (Matt. 2:13). This demonstrated his genuine love for Jesus and the preservation of His future—the call of God on His life.

We should not overlook these acts of love because they played an invaluable role in the spiritual formation of our Lord. The role of parents in the spiritual shaping of their children is to create a home environment that makes it easy for the child to locate and remain on the path of the divine. Mary and Joseph did that, and with God's help so can you.

God wants to use you

In *My Utmost for His Highest* J. Oswald Chambers writes: "The bedrock of Christianity is repentance. Strictly speaking, a man cannot repent when he chooses; repentance is a gift of God. The old Puritans used to pray for 'the gift of tears.' If ever you cease to know the virtue of repentance, you are in darkness. Examine yourself and see if you have forgotten how to be sorry."[2] God uses people who've adjusted their behavior and perspective through repentance.

Once you realize that you've fallen short on your goal to build a home life conducive to solid spiritual formation, don't beat yourself up. Simply repent. Turn around! Refocus on the original goal and go after it. Repentance is a key to unlock your private prison of shame, guilt, and self-condemnation. Repentance is a game changer; it is a defining moment.

Repentance only happens when you renew your convictions. Conviction is sight from within. It's not fuzzy or ambiguous! Your priorities have become crystal clear. You are now willing to fight for the desired spiritual state of your family. Conviction is the fuel for a warrior spirit! When there's conviction, you don't wait for others to agree with your timing, need, or desperate state—you just act upon what deeply troubles you. The spiritual state of your family weighs heavily on your heart, and you've decided to do something about it. The best move you could possibly make at this point is to reset your spiritual life.

John Chrysostom, an early church father, said, "Repentance is a medicine which destroys sin, a gift bestowed from heaven, an admirable virtue, a grace exceeding the power of laws."[3] The value and power of repentance helped one young mother decide to make a clean break from the imprisonment of her dysfunctional family background. As I sat in a service many years ago, I recall a lady giving this personal testimony: "It wasn't until I realized that we don't walk backward, so I had to stop living in the past and make positive and inspirational changes walking forward into my future." This is what I'm asking you to do if your past is haunting you. Make today the first day of the rest of your parenting life. Forgive yourself. Repent and make a clean break into God's bright future for you and your kids.

The significance of having a proper attitude became brutally important when a lady challenged a youth group to repent of their ungodly outlook on a missions trip. The missions team was in Kentucky working on a poor woman's house. They started with her yard.

Her yard had old cars, broken-down sofas, rusty bicycles, and garbage strewn all over the front yard. The porch had piles of other junk and irreparable things. The youth group hated every minute of it. The sight of it made them cynical. They started making sarcastic remarks to one another; they argued, teased, and kept making digs at one another. Their behavior was horrible.

After a day or two of this, the lady of the house finally came out with tears streaming down her face. She told the youth group to sit on the grass, in the one place that was fairly clean. Then she let them have it. "Don't you know I've been praying for God to send someone to help me?...Don't you know that you are the answer to my prayers? Why don't you treat each other like the answer to prayer?"

More tears streamed down her face as she pleaded with them.

Their attitude shifted at that moment. They changed how they saw one another. They saw themselves as answers to prayer.[4]

As this illustration shows, repentance is indeed a game changer. It renews our values, perspective, and behavior. Chrysostom is right. Repentance is a gift bestowed from heaven.

ACTION STEPS

As you teach your kids how to pray, forgive yourself of any poor practices that keep you living in the past. Acknowledge the following tips to help you take the step toward freedom.

- It is God's will that my family thrives spiritually.

- Repentance is being sorry for my sins and deciding to quit committing them.

Pray this prayer:

Lord, please forgive me for not being the parent You've called me to be. Help me to make a clean start today. Give me wisdom to understand my children, to know when to be silent, and to create a home environment where they can grow spiritually. I ask You this in Jesus's name. Amen.

Chapter 4

LITTLE JOHNNY
(A.K.A. JOHN THE BAPTIST)

———— ☼ ————

IN THE THIRTY years I've been a pastor, I have seen thousands of children come to the Lord. Many of them were born from married couples who longed for their birth. Others were adopted through foster care programs or private agencies. And some were the result of unplanned and unwanted pregnancies.

Regardless of how they got here, children have one thing in common: the need for a loving home. Even if you attend the best church with the godliest people in town, your child will languish spiritually without a nurturing home. I have seen it all too many times. No lessons a church teaches on prayer will hold up without building the foundation that anchors this sacred discipline.

That truth is emphasized by the following story:

The typical after-dinner walk with James and his wife, Penny, was pleasantly interrupted one evening when they met a ten-year-old boy named Billy. He came racing down the path and almost crashed into them, shouting, "Dad, where's Amy?" He had mistaken James for his dad. "Sir, I'm sorry. I thought you were my dad."

"It's OK, son," James said, "we all make mistakes." As the little boy turned and walked away, the happy couple couldn't help notice his limp and some of his features. He definitely had Down's syndrome.

In a few seconds the boy ran back and announced: "My name is Billy. Can I give you both a hug? You have been so nice to me."

Billy hugged them tightly and shared, "You're my new friends. I want you to know that I'll be praying for you." As soon as he released them, he said, "I got to go. God bless you!"

James and Penny, tearing up, just gazed at Billy as he limped off to play with his sister. After Billy went down the slide, his mother walked over and gave him a big hug. He was obviously a special child to her.[1]

Sometimes God uses the Billys of the world to break down our lives to one common denominator. A child who lives in a loving home will thrive regardless of her natural limitations. You don't need a perfect child or even a perfect home. There is no such thing—at least not in this life. You do need a loving home!

Consider John the Baptist, the forerunner of Jesus, as a good example of an intercessor. His life of prayer did not begin in adulthood, however. It began when he was a child. His family wasn't perfect, but they were emotionally healthy. It's encouraging to know that kids can have rich spiritual lives even at a tender age. Equally encouraging is the fact that imperfect people living in imperfect homes can train children in the art of prayer.

TRAINING AMIDST PROBLEMS

John was the only child of Zechariah, a priest, and his wife, Elizabeth. For most of their married life Elizabeth was barren. John came long after his parents had lost hope of ever having a child. One day, when Zechariah was at work, the angel Gabriel visited him and said God was going to give him and Elizabeth a son—an answer to a prayer decades old. The birth of John was a gift to his mom and dad. He was their "miracle baby." He was their "love child." He was their "little bundle of joy gift-wrapped by God Himself." Imagine how often John probably heard the story of Gabriel's visit. Gabriel's appearance wasn't some random moment of happenstance. The angel came at the most climactic moment in Zechariah's career—just as he was about to offer incense on the golden altar (Luke 1:9). An individual priest could only offer the incense on the golden altar in the holy place *once* in his lifetime because there were so many priests (about eighteen thousand at the time of Christ).[2] As Zechariah was serving faithfully, in the face of his delayed dream for a son, Gabriel appeared and announced the news. A miracle child was going to be naturally conceived and born by this chosen couple.

God showed up at the most unexpected time, yet it was the right time.

If we put ourselves in Elizabeth's place, we can see how John's spiritual life might have shaped up. Barrenness in the first century was viewed as a curse and carried a huge social stigma. Yet Elizabeth was not bitter, because she guarded her heart. Her name means "God of fullness; God is plenty." Her barrenness did not cause her to despise her name or become cynical toward God.

Elizabeth kept her problem in perspective. She reasoned that life and marriage are bigger than having or not having children. She stayed positive and enthusiastic about the things He *had* given her. She knew God's faithfulness, love, and mercy. When Elizabeth finally became pregnant, she said: "The Lord has done this for me....In these days he has shown his favor and taken away my disgrace among the people" (Luke 1:25, NIV).

In the French Pyrenees there is a shrine that attracts a lot of people who are in need of healing. They come there to pray for a miracle. On one particular evening, after the close of World War II, a one-legged man hobbled down the street to the shrine. Some onlookers made fun of him and said, "Does he think God is going to give him back his leg?" The traveler overhead them and replied that he didn't expect God to give him back his leg. He said, "I'm going to pray to God to help me to live without it!"[3]

"What then are we to do about our problems? We must learn to live with them until such time as God delivers us from them," writes twentieth-century preacher A. W. Tozer. "If we cannot remove them, then we must pray for grace to endure them without murmuring. Problems patiently endured will work for our spiritual perfecting. They harm us only when we resist them or endure them unwillingly."[4] Both Zechariah and Elizabeth knew this. Their practice shaped the home in which John was born, grew up, and learned the ways of God. It's not always easy, but we must strive to do the same.

PARENTING A SPIRITUAL CHAMPION

Some kids seem to emerge from the womb as ready-made champions. That's how we see them. And what compounds this mystique, placing them in a rarified air, is that they are biblical characters. When God chooses to do that, it leads me to make a connection with our modern-day judicial system. Sometimes a judge chooses to seal the records of a minor. The sealed record creates more mystery and intrigue. Such is the case with John the Baptist.

Similar to Jesus, the biblical narrative shows John having a bigger-than-life birth. It then skips to his adult-hood, where we see scores of people coming to him to be water baptized for their sins. It begs the questions: *What do we know about his childhood? How did his parents train him in the things of God? What were his prayer habits?* The records are sealed tight. God allowed a little peek into John's childhood in a single verse: "And the child grew and became strong in spirit; and he lived in the wilderness until he appeared publicly to Israel" (Luke 1:80, NIV). This verse reveals three secrets about how Little Johnny became a praying boy and ultimately became a man of prayer.

First secret: maturity is a process

Growth does not occur overnight. John did not become this tremendous man of prayer suddenly. Spiritual lessons and habits take time to develop before proficiency sets in. As a parent, if you approach your role as a life-long job, that alone brings a sense of hope. It lightens the pressure, which is often self-induced.

When I fly to distant places like Malaysia, New Zealand, or Thailand—places on the other side of the world from New Jersey—the flight becomes doable once I tell myself, "I'm going to be on this airplane for fifteen to twenty hours." Before I step onto the aircraft, take my seat, and soar to some thirty-five thousand feet above sea level for twenty hours, I first take a long-term view. If I don't, "air rage" is certain to set in. In the early days of my ministry I would board the plane in a hurry to land. The flights back then, though the same length of time, felt like an eternity. They don't feel that way now. The only change was my attitude. Weeks before the trip I start readying myself by acknowledging that the flight is long and I must accept that reality. I plan for it by bringing books to read that

I'll relish. I even pack good headphones to thoroughly enjoy the in-flight movies.

We need the same approach to help our children develop good prayer habits. It will take them time—much time—to learn how to pray. If we're impatient with them, they may interpret this to mean God is impatient.

Prayer, like other spiritual disciplines, requires clarity in your child's understanding, and yours. You must be clear about your relationship with God—what He expects from you and what you expect from Him. Your child must also have this clarity. It's tough enough for us adults to gain such clearheadedness. Getting to this stage is daunting, especially for children who have underdeveloped reasoning skills (which will last through their early twenties). Children are observing thousands of new things each day. And they are figuring out how to react to them, what level of priority to give them, and what is considered an acceptable result by the people who are important to them. There is a lot to absorb.

A recent YouTube post quickly went viral. It shows a toddler screaming and attempting to run away from his shadow. The kid doesn't understand what a shadow is and that it never leaves him. So this dark silhouette that is inescapable may be cute to us, but it's frightening to the child. New things take time to understand and figure out, especially for our little ones.

When it comes to prayer, we can't place unrealistic expectations on a child. If we do, they will learn to hate praying, or they will pray only out of obligation in a mechanical way, just as the Pharisees in the Bible did. Pharisees were the strictest of the Jewish sects. Jesus often chided and openly rebuked them because of their pretentious practices. Their prayers weren't sincere or authentic. These often rote exercises were staged for others to see and admire. Jesus taught that God paid them no mind when they prayed (Matt. 6:5). We don't want to create those kinds of young Christ followers. If your kids develop a negative feeling about prayer, they may deflect their negative feelings toward God.

In his book *The Purple Pig and Other Miracles* Dick Eastman tells the story of Benny, a fifteen-year-old teenager who had the mind of a six-year-old. During a testimony service Benny interrupted the service as he testified before the congregation:

> "I love you all very much. It's true that I can't get a job like other boys my age. I can't even go to a real school like all of you. At my school we just make baskets. But I can love you."
>
> Wiping away his tears, Benny added, "And I can pray for you. Just remember; if you get discouraged, Benny is praying for you. It's not much, but it's all I can do. I'll be praying. Anybody can pray.'"[5]

I'm sure the patience extended to Benny helped him develop good prayer habits and the confidence that when he prayed, God would answer him.

Second secret: spiritual maturity is also a process

To understand how little kids, and more particularly Little Johnny, developed a prayer life, let's refer again to Luke 1:80, which says: "And the child grew and became *strong in spirit*" (NIV, emphasis added). The Jerusalem Bible reads: "Meanwhile the child grew up and his spirit matured." Apart from John's physical maturation his spirit matured. He recognized and applied himself to things that promoted spiritual growth. Spiritual growth and natural growth don't run on the same tracks. They are completely independent processes. There are a lot of adult Christians who are still spiritual babies despite many years in the kingdom of God. Their infantile spirituality usually comes from a neglect of activities and disciplines that promote spiritual growth.

Spiritual babies seldom make a commitment to having daily devotionals, participating in ministry activities, sharing their faith with unbelievers, or even attending church regularly. These habits directly correlate with one's spiritual growth. For instance, the 2014 General Social Survey showed a slight growth over three decades in the number of Americans who pray at least once a day. The latest figure was 57 percent, up from 54 percent in 1983. However, for those who attended weekly religious services, the data showed the daily prayer practice soared to almost nine in ten Americans.[6] Spiritual maturity is a process that is inextricably linked to applying ourselves to proven habits. This survey proves that.

As a child John became spiritually mature through discipline. Growth is not the result of knowing Bible stories. Spiritual growth occurs by *doing* the same things the heroes of our faith did. Little Johnny applied himself to the principles and practices of the Old Testament giants. As an adult he was asked by the priests and Levites, "'Are you Elijah?' He said 'I am not.'" (John 1:21). The priests and Levites then asked, "Are you the Prophet?" His reply was, "No" (John 1:21). John knew the stories surrounding these heroes of the faith. More importantly he practiced the disciplines they employed. John's followers spent time fasting and praying (Matt. 9:14), and it's likely they were following his example. Because of the limited passages showcasing John's childhood, I cannot definitively say that he fasted as a child. But I can convincingly say that fasting and prayer are two of the disciplines that make one *strong in spirit*.

I am not suggesting any kind of fasting for children. At this age it is enough to simply help your child learn how to connect their prayers with the Bible and how to develop a regular life of prayer that leads to a growing relationship with Christ. The practice of fasting will become organic as they mature. Some may venture to fast as teenagers. Even if they never fast until they become adults, it must be their choice and theirs alone if it is going to have any spiritual merit.

My point is that Little Johnny understood spiritual growth and was courageous enough to practice certain habits. We teach toddlers to say grace before each meal. This practice was a requirement for the Ireland household, even the little members. I've discovered that rules without reason produce rebellion. We spent time explaining the reasoning behind this rule. We shared the pertinent Bible passages so that their faith would rest in the Scriptures and not solely in the desires or practices of their parents.

Our daughters learned that saying grace demonstrated our thankfulness to God for His provision. Saying grace allowed us the opportunity to express our gratitude and appreciation for the food. It was also a way for us to offer blessings for the ones who prepared the meal. It took time for that spiritual discipline to stick. Sometimes they'd forget and start chowing down. If I was in a sarcastic frame of mind, I would say something to the effect: "We're not wolves!" After their little snickering died down, I would ask one of them to give thanks.

Without proper parental or spiritual guidance in place, children will stumble in their discovery of the secrets that promote discipleship growth. With a good role model in place, the process becomes more streamlined. This makes for quicker results. John had good role models. His parents knew patience and the power of prayer, and they had walked with God during good times and bad.

Third secret: solitude is a good thing

The single verse we have to draw from to understand the spiritual formation of Little Johnny reads:

> And the child grew and became strong in spirit; *and he lived in the wilderness* until he appeared publicly to Israel.
>
> —LUKE 1:80, NIV, EMPHASIS ADDED

We learn that John spent time in solitude as part of his preparation for ministry. The Bible is silent as to when exactly he left his parent's home in the hill country of Judea (Luke 1:39) to go into the wilderness of Judea. What we can understand from this text is that solitude was part of his lifestyle.

Solitude is not punishment. It is the voluntary pulling aside from ordinary affairs, which may include human contact, for short terms in order to seek the Lord. I love what Richard Foster says about solitude in his book *Celebration of Discipline*: "Inward solitude has outward manifestations. There is the freedom to be alone, not in order to be away from people but in order to hear the divine Whisper better."[7]

All the great Bible heroes intentionally spent some alone time for the purpose of seeking God in prayer. Moses did it. He spent forty days and forty nights in prayer and fasting. The result was phenomenal. He received the Ten Commandments—the moral and ethical code that guides the legal system for most societies, even to this day (Exod. 34:28).

Jesus also spent forty days and forty nights in solitude as He fasted and prayed. The outcome was the launching of His earthly ministry (Luke 4:1–2). Paul, the great apostle and principal architect of most of the New Testament letters, spent some time in Arabia for the sole purpose of seeking God (Gal. 1:15–17). Seeking God during times of solitude allows us to pray, as Ruth Haley Barton writes:

> Holy One, there is something I wanted to tell you, but there have been errands to run, bills to pay, meetings to attend, washing to do…and I forget what it is I wanted to say to you, and forget what I am about or why. Oh God, don't forget me please, for the sake of Jesus Christ.[8]

As an adult I see the need for intentional moments of solitude. You may not be able to take forty days and go to the nearby desert or a Marriott hotel. But perhaps you can take a day trip or a four-hour break from the busyness of life to seek the One whom you love so deeply.

Your child needs to learn how to appreciate the value of solitude as well. Our kids are always busy. From ballet practice we shuffle them off to drama rehearsal. Or if you have athletes, they're running to soccer, football, or baseball practice. And when they are home, they're joined at the hip—or should I say, at the fingertips—to the latest tech gadget. This modern tech age can cripple spiritual development. It keeps kids stressed out, wired up, and disconnected from God.

Certainly God is omnipresent. He's everywhere at once. He's with them on the baseball field, on the ballet floor, or in the rehearsal room for the big school play. But He's often not on their radar. Your little ones need to have moments of solitude, just as you do. They need to have moments of solitude to get in touch with their own thoughts, heart, desires, and then the thoughts, heart, and desires of God. The Dutch theologian Henri Nouwen observed: "Solitude is an essential element for the spiritual health of a child. If we only stimulate our children—keep them busy with endless stories with no space to be alone—that's not good."[9]

Let's take a play from the playbook of Little Johnny to help teach our children to pray:

> *Lord, I've been so busy with homework, play dates, and keeping up with my friends that I feel empty. I've even lost sight of what You've been speaking to my heart. Dear God, renew my desires to get to know You better. Forgive me for allowing my life to crowd You out. Help me to serve Jesus even while I'm a kid.*

To foster times of solitude that are realistic for a child, start with having times of "no tech toys or gadgets." I know some families that created house rules where all gadgets must be docked in a central place at 8:00 p.m. during the school week. This created space for family time, quiet times, and uninterrupted moments to reflect on their day. These families framed this downtime in such a way that it did not appear punitive or excessive.

Again, depending on the age and maturity of your children, you might want to add other components to this downtime so that it captures a genuine sense of solitude. These periods should have built-in components that tie it to connecting or reconnecting with God. The television is off. The cell phone is docked and muted. The Bible is open. Perhaps worship music that your kids like is playing in the background as they learn to focus their minds on God. Similar to all other disciplines, solitude is a muscle that needs to be developed. If you've never spent extended moments in solitude, it may seem torturous at first.

Start slow. You might block out fifteen minutes. Once they master that, increase it to thirty minutes. Keep doing this until they are able to enjoy a large block of uninterrupted time to connect with God. Solitude creates a respite from the fast-paced world. It's like someone who comes out of the heavy rain to stand under a protective store awning.

Solitude allows us to catch our breath. This pause enables reflection and an opportunity to thank God for His goodness. Daily activities have a way of keeping us going on many levels. Beyond the physical drain there is an emotional and spiritual one. The emptiness feeds into existing stress, which triggers short tempers and strained relationships. I'm sure you've noticed that your kids get cranky when they are tired. It puts the entire household in a funk.

Solitude deepens our relationship with God and conveys that we want to hear what He's speaking to our hearts. Little Johnny intentionally spent time in the desert of Judea to hear from God. He needed clarity of purpose. It emboldened him, as it will you and your kids. Clarity will also heighten your sense of courage and sharpen your focus. Without it you are tossed here and there by every fleeting thought or exciting idea that comes your way.

ACTION STEPS

As you forge ahead in the process of training your kids how to pray, invite God into your home life by drawing some lessons from John the Baptist. We learned that:

- Having problems doesn't disqualify you from raising spiritual champions.

- Maturity is a process. It requires practicing patience with your child.

Pray this prayer:

Lord, help me to keep my problems in per-
spective. I place them on Your altar right now.
Please help me to solve them. In the mean-
time give me the strength to always have the
right attitude so that I'm never defeated by
these problems. Help me to rely totally on
Your grace so that my home is a peaceful and
enjoyable place to live and raise my children. I
ask you this in Jesus's name. Amen.

Chapter 5

UNLOCKING KID POWER

———— ✸ ————

PEDIATRICIAN DAVID CERQUEIRA shared a story of how a dying girl showed his church the honor of serving God:

One particular Sunday his wife prepared a lesson for her Sunday school class on how everyone can be useful and that usefulness is serving God. The kids quietly listened, soaking up her words. As the lesson ended, a little girl named Sarah spoke up: "Teacher, what can I do? I don't know how to do many useful things."

Surprised by her question, the teacher thought for a moment and then thoughtfully gave what would become an unforgettable answer. She noticed an empty flower vase on the windowsill and told Sarah she could bring in a flower for the vase. "That would be a very useful thing," she said.

"But that's not important," Sarah said, while frowning.

"It is," the teacher replied, "if you are helping someone."

From then on, Sarah brought in a flower and put it in the vase each Sunday. She did this without a single reminder or a word of encouragement. The pastor heard about Sarah's faithfulness, and he placed the vase in the main sanctuary for all to see. That Sunday he delivered a sermon on the honor of serving others. Sarah's vase was a terrific example and visual, and the congregation was moved by the message.

During that same week Sarah's mother called the pediatrician, Dr. Cerqueira. She was worried because Sarah did not have an appetite and had less energy than normal. The doctor scheduled a visit the next day. Sarah endured several tests and examinations. The results were heartbreaking. She had leukemia.

Because of the pediatrician's relationship with the family, he felt the best way to break this painful news to Sarah's parents was face-to-face. He stopped by their house on the way home. They all sat at Sarah's family's kitchen table as the doctor explained how Sarah's genetics and the leukemia formed a horrible mix. There was nothing that could be done medically to save Sarah's life.

As time went on, Sarah became confined to her bed. This little girl who used to be full of life lost her smile. She lost a lot of weight too. A day came when Sarah hardly moved. The doctor knew Sarah wouldn't live much longer.

That Sunday, during the sermon, the pastor suddenly stopped speaking. With a shocked look on his face he stared at the back of the church. Standing there was Sarah! She was wrapped in a blanket and was holding a dandelion.

To everyone's surprise, Sarah slowly walked to the front of the church where her vase still sat by the pulpit. She put her flower in the vase and a piece of paper beside it. The congregation sat watching little Sarah place her flower in the vase for the last time.

In four days Sarah died.

The doctor later received the note Sarah had left by the flower. In pink crayon Sarah had written:

> Dear God,
> This vase has been the biggest honor of my life.
> —Sarah

Serving God is, as Sarah put it, "the biggest honor" of all.[1]

Kid power is very real and quite formidable. Sarah is not an exception. The impact of her feat became public because someone paid attention to her. The same can happen to your child. When we examine the prayer lives of Jesus and John the Baptist, we see that God welcomes children into His throne room. Throughout church history kids have stirred the faith of the church as they did their part to advance the cause of Christ. Kid power is unlocked when they learn how to pray.

God's throne room is not cordoned off to little visitors, as some living rooms are to the children of the house. The throne room is not a showcase where we go to sightsee or take pictures. It's a place where mercy and grace are extended at the request of some penitent soul (Heb. 4:16). Transactions of this nature are often messy. The cry for mercy is not the most articulate, because the heart is usually broken up. The words, at times, are not even coherent. But God understands them because He listens to hearts, not necessarily words.

After thirty years of counseling people at their worst moments, I've observed something consistent. When husbands and wives ask one another for forgiveness, it's seldom without tears. The events that brought them to that place are very painful. Their selfish actions broke their spouse's heart in pieces. And now they see it. I've seen lips quiver, speech become slurred, and voices crack as spouses asked for forgiveness. Sometimes the words were unclear, but the body language and tearful hearts were anything but. The appeals for forgiveness were authentic. In those moments the plea was received without hesitation. Forgiveness freely flowed.

I'm convinced that God does the same thing when little ones come into His throne room. Their flubs are overlooked because of the sincerity of their hearts. In our Sunday school classes we encourage kids to pray. One particular Sunday Joan asked two kids to pray over the offering. The moment she pointed to Teddy, he excitedly began to pray. This five-year-old first cleared his throat and then went into a dramatic deep voice as he said, "Heavenly Father." He continued for quite some time, praying for families and then the offering, all with his best baritone imitation. When it was Sally's turn, she prayed, "Lord, bless the offering because the church needs it to buy things. The church buys us lots of fruit snacks and we really like them. Also Lord, bless Elmo and all my Sesame Street friends. We thank you for all of them in Jesus's name. Amen."

When I heard the story, I chuckled. I'm not sure why Teddy seems to think that prayer needed a deep and serious tone of voice. I'm sure, however, that his contrived voice won't prevent his access to God's throne room. Neither is the throne room closed to Sally because her childlike mind wants God to bless fictitious characters from Sesame Street.

Joan told me about other prayers the kids prayed. One little girl said, "God, help my daddy to stop using drugs." Another five-year-old asked the class to pray for his school friend who was going to have surgery next week. Even at a young age our children understand that life is too difficult to go it alone. They need God's help just as much as we do. Kid power is just as formidable as that of adults. On bended knees we are all equal. Through prayer we are able to ask almighty God for help.

Prayer gives us access to His omnipotence. The neglect of prayer is to turn our backs on the greatest power source known to humanity—God. Conversely, when we engage in prayer, we turn on the greatest power source. Prayer gives our kids access to God's limitless authority. This power cannot be hindered by anyone, regardless of their title or position. It is unstoppable. That's why it's critical that you teach your kids how to pray. Kid power happens when they connect to divine power. Don't make their age an issue. God doesn't!

The famed nineteenth-century French priest John Vianney shared: "My little children, your hearts are small, but prayer stretches them and makes them capable of loving God. Through prayer we receive a foretaste of heaven and something of paradise comes down upon us. Prayer never leaves us without sweetness. It is honey that flows into the souls and makes all things sweet. When we pray properly, sorrows disappear like snow before the sun."[2] Every generation must come to the realization that children have great power on bended knees.

Consider young Samuel. As a boy he had a life-transforming encounter with God. The Lord showed him that the aging high priest Eli would not live much longer because he had failed to restrain his two adult sons and was lax in disciplining them. They were wicked and contemptible (1 Sam. 2:12). Samuel's prophetic word to Eli shaped Israel's history. Eli and his two sons died, and the ark of the covenant was taken from Israel in battle (1 Sam. 4).

Imagine a young boy being used by the Holy Spirit to communicate God's historic judgment against an erring priest. As a child, Samuel became known as a prophet (1 Sam. 3:19–21). Kid power was at work in and through him. This prophecy given to Eli was not the only one God used young Samuel to deliver. We don't usually see kids going around making predictions in the name of God. This role is not the norm for kids, but it could be if we took them more seriously. The fact that the Bible gives us glimpses of kid power is a strong indication that children are not too young to have power on bended knees.

Children need our encouragement to spur them along this path of intimacy with God. Our praise helps them recognize their value. This is exactly what the Sunday school teacher did for Sarah—the little girl stricken with leukemia. In the case of Samuel, his growth did not happen in a vacuum. Eli was a tremendous encourager. Amid his faults Eli nurtured the call of God on Samuel's life through encouragement. The Scripture says that "the boy ministered to the LORD before Eli the priest" (1 Sam. 2:11). Eli took Samuel under his wing. He gave young Samuel important tasks to perform. This helped little Samuel see and recognize his value. Apart from caring for the basic needs of the old priest, Samuel would daily open the doors of the house of the Lord (1 Sam. 3:15). This is what kids want. They want to know what they're tasked to do has value.

More importantly, they want to know that they are important to you. By allowing Samuel to care for him, the old man helped the boy recognize his value. The care was not simply running errands; it included just hanging out together. Do you know the feelings little kids have when they know you like them? All good mentor-protégé relationships are built on friendship and not just authority or knowledge.

THE IMPORTANCE OF VALUE

Value speaks of worth. An anonymous source once shared a story that appeared in the old *Moody Monthly* about a restaurant visit by Craig Massey, the popular Christian author. Massey heard an angry father say to his seven-year-old son, "What good are you?" Having just accidentally spilled his glass of milk, the kid hangs his head and answered, "Nothing."

Fast-forward years later, and Massey recalled being disgusted with his own son after a seemingly insignificant incident. He heard himself ask what he called "the cruelest of questions a father can ask." He fired off the same kind of question: "What are you good for anyway?" Like the boy in the restaurant, his son replied, "Nothing." Immediately Massey was convicted by his cruel question. As he thought it over, he recognized that the question was reasonable but the answer was not. Several days later when his son blew it again with another minor offense, Massey asked, "What are you good for?" This time, before the boy could answer, he hugged him and kissed him and said: "I'll tell you what you're good for. You're good for loving!"

This became a standing response whenever Massey asked his boy, "What are you good for?" His son would say, "I'm good for loving."[3] Imagine how your child's self-esteem and confidence soar knowing their value is not based on performance or achievements. Raising powerful praying kids is directly tied to building up their self-esteem and value.

Offer value

Our kids get their sense of value from the people who love them. Just as Massey was able to skillfully turn his initial harsh response into a positive one, you can do the same. The primary source of value has to come from the most significant figure in your child's life. This means that mom and dad are incredibly important during the formative years. Later, outsiders will provide added value to your child's self-esteem and dignity. But in the early days you're the principal value-maker. No matter how great the church, you still must see yourself as the "rain-maker" for the sense of value your child needs.

Praise more than you criticize

A child's self-esteem is directly related to the ratio of praise and criticism he receives. Even if criticism is spoken in a sweet tone, it's still criticism and can dent the child's sense of worth. Since you are the primary authority figure in your child's life, he looks to you for validation.

Find things to praise your child about, no matter what. If she cleaned her room, praise her. Even if it's not to your full satisfaction, praise her for the effort. You may even come alongside of her and say, "Sweetheart, I'm proud of the great job you did. It's really tough to put all these toys away. I can help you with the rest." In other words, find a way to boost her sense of worth. When she goes to pray, she will know that God values her too.

Engage in your child's activities

Children need to see you engaged in their world. Inviting them to pray or to learn how to pray cannot be a one-sided thing. You're asking them to learn something that seems, at least at first, like an adult activity. From their little minds, prayer is something *you* like to do. They see it as *your thing*. To help broaden their view, enter into their activities with equal enthusiasm and zeal. Don't wait for them to introduce the topic; you take the lead. Showing interest in their sport or after-school activity will demonstrate that you see value in what they do.

I remember when my daughter Jessica was about eight years old and was into having her fingernails painted. One evening when her older sister and mother weren't at home, she brought me into her world. The conversation started off when she said, "Dads can't do what moms do!" She baited me. With my type-A personality I was not going to back down from a challenge. I replied, "I can do whatever your mother can do!" She threw out a number of things, from sewing to braiding hair, to which I replied, "I can do that." Finally she said, "I bet you can't paint fingernails." I said, "Get your fingernail polish!" She returned in a split second with all of her nail polishing stuff.

We sat on my bed, and I painted her nails, trying my best not to get any of the polish on her skin. After I finished both hands, I said, "I told you I can do whatever your mom can do." I forgot all about it. When Sunday rolled around, I was holding Jessica's hand as we walked through the church hallway to get to the sanctuary. One of the ladies happened to see Jessica's fingernail polish and said, "Your nails look beautiful." Jessica stopped and held out her hand, nails up, so the lady could really get a good look.

The lady asked, "Who did your nails?" I was so embarrassed at what was to follow. My little girl didn't even hesitate to blurt out, "Daddy did!" The lady looked at me, her pastor—the man of God—and simply smiled. It's been about fifteen years since that time, but I still can't shake the uneasiness of being exposed as Jessica's manicurist. Seriously, my participation in this activity simply conveyed to my daughter that I was *all in* as a dad. She was not a bother to me. Her activities were of interest to me, even the ones that did not come natural to me. So when it came to prayer, she had no trouble following my lead.

Consider the opposite—when a kid sees himself as a bother or a pest. Charles Francis Adams, the nineteenth-century political figure and diplomat, kept a diary. One day he logged this entry: "Went fishing with my son today—a day wasted." His son, Brook Adams, also kept a diary, which is still in existence. On that same day Brook made this entry: "Went fishing with my father—the most wonderful day of my life!"[4] The father thought he was wasting his time, while his son saw it as an opportunity to connect and build friendship with his dad. Can you imagine how Brook would have felt had he read his father's entry for that day? It would have crushed him.

MAXIMIZE THE ORDINARY MOMENTS

Spiritual instructions best occur in ordinary moments. This is why God said to the Israelites:

> Therefore you must fix these words of mine in your heart and in your soul, and bind them as a sign on your hand, so that they may be as frontlets between your eyes. You shall teach them to your children, speaking of them when you sit in your house and when you walk by the way, when you lie down, and when you rise up.
> —DEUTERONOMY 11:18–19

When you draw spiritual lessons from the ordinary affairs of life, it shows that God is involved in everything. He is not just the "Sunday morning" God that we only visit during weekly worship. He's the God of the entire week, even when we're driving to the mall or the soccer game.

I recently learned that my wife used to periodically pray with our youngest daughter when she drove her to school. As Jessica shared her challenges or interests, Marlinda would say, "Let's pray now about those things." She was teaching Jessica how to pray about the affairs of her day and her life. Today Jessica is an adult. Last year she and Marlinda went to a women's conference together. Knowing that there were quite a number of mother-daughter groups present, the speaker invited the daughters to share with their mom one of their most enjoyable childhood moments together. Jessica told Marlinda that she enjoyed the moments they prayed together in the car going to school. Marlinda did not know those ordinary moments had such a profound effect on Jessica.

This is precisely why God instructed us to use life's ordinary moments as teaching opportunities for our kids. As long as it's not forced, scripted, or overwhelming, the opportunity can prove to be something special and memorable for both of you.

Limit the teaching moment.

The most powerful teaching moments are just that, a moment—a short span of time. It shouldn't feel like an eternity. It should be special, like a snack. Eating an entire strawberry cheesecake is not a special treat if it's a daily occurrence. That's not even considered snacking. It's gluttony! A slice or two is a snack, but not an entire twelve-inch gourmet cheesecake with all of the fixings.

Allow the Holy Spirit to lead you even in these mundane things. If your child seems uncomfortable or if you sense resistance, just change direction. Wait for a more opportune time to offer a spiritual lesson. You may share it at a time when you sense the inspiration of the Holy Spirit in a stronger way. If God gives you some insight about a spiritual truth, even in the middle of a very basic task, that is likely your best opportunity. Go for it!

Leland Wang, the Chinese evangelist, shared an incident from his childhood that vividly illustrates the work of Christ. On one occasion he had been very naughty, and his mother, with a stick in her hand, called him to her to be punished. But he ran off, taunting her because she could not catch him. She had little chance of catching her small, lively son.

So she stood still and said, "I feel ashamed of myself that I have brought up a boy who is not willing to be disciplined by his mother when he does wrong, so I must punish myself," and she began to whip her bare arm. This so touched Leland's heart that he ran back to his mother, threw himself into her arms, and pleaded with her not to hurt herself but to punish him, but no further punishment was necessary.

Leland says that, as he grew older, this memory helped him to understand the great love of the Lord Jesus Christ who willingly took our place on the cross.[5]

Keep the goal in mind.

The teaching moment is not for you. It is for your children. Eli's affirmation of Samuel was for Samuel's benefit. Keep this as your goal, or the teaching moment will quickly become dysfunctional and weird. Can you imagine Eli having some self-talk in the back room that went like this: "Boy, I really felt good about that teaching moment. I learned a lot. I always like trying out my sermon on the kid." If something like that did happen, Eli would not have been the encourager Scripture makes him out to be.

The purpose of the moment was for Samuel. An example of this is the first time Samuel heard the voice of God. At first he thought it was Eli calling him. He jumped up from his bed at the sound of his name and ran to Eli, saying, "Here I am" (1 Sam. 3:4). Not realizing what was going on, the old man told Samuel, "I did not call. Return, lie down again" (1 Sam. 3:5). This happened three times that evening. Each time Samuel ran to Eli. After the third occurrence Eli recognized what was going on. He seized the occasion for a quick teaching moment. He told young Samuel, "Go, lie down. And it will be, if He calls you, that you will say, 'Speak, LORD, for Your servant listens'" (1 Sam. 3:9). Samuel did what his mentor suggested.

Notice how Eli limited his instructions to the matter at hand. God was trying to get ahold of Samuel. The main thing in this teachable moment was to get Samuel to position himself to hear the voice of God. Eli simply said that he should listen and then respond, "Speak, Lord. Your servant is listening." Eli kept the main thing the main thing. He did not clutter the moment with a dissertation on hearing the voice of God. The wise leader did not even try to frighten Samuel into thinking that it may be the voice of a demon or a psychological disorder. Or perhaps the kid was just too exhausted and was hallucinating. Eli kept the teachable moment simple and uncluttered. The moment was for Samuel and not anyone else. Strive to do the same with your child.

Keep the moment positive

Teachable moments are precious when the lesson is positive and enlightening. In fact, the word *speaking,* as used in Deuteronomy 11:19, rarely has any connection with destructive speech. It is a natural conversation—an enjoyable talk. You'll know it's effective when your child starts asking questions and giving feedback. This shows that he's engaged.

Once these moments sound like a lecture, your child will simply detach and will soon come to despise these occasions. If your voice deepens like that of five-year-old Teddy when he prays, you're signaling to your child: "We're now going to have a *teachable moment about God.*" Once he notices the change in your pitch, he'll turn a deaf ear, because it's clear to him you're about to lunge into a religious speech. Teachable moments benefit the child. Spiritual reprimands benefit you.

If you notice that your special moment is becoming a lecture, stop. Change the subject to something more pleasant. Pray about it later before bringing it up again. Ask God for strategy and insight to better introduce the subject to your child. Taking the needed time to bathe it in prayer is using wisdom and shows that you believe God cares about the spiritual welfare of your child.

Referring back to Eli and Samuel, the old priest successfully created an atmosphere where a kid like Samuel could excel spiritually. You can do the same. Eli conveyed value and importance to Samuel's role. This perspective bled into forming a positive orientation when it came to his hosting teachable moments. Don't misunderstand. Eli had some tough moments with Samuel. One in particular was the morning after God spoke to Samuel for the first time. Eli called the boy and asked, "What is the thing that the LORD has spoken to you?" Before Samuel could answer, Eli warned, "Do not hide it from me. Thus may God do so to you, and more also, if you hide from me a word out of all the things that He spoke to you" (1 Sam. 3:17).

Please remember that Eli did not discipline his wicked sons. And God was set on punishing him for that blatant neglect, which brought great harm to the priesthood and Israel. Talk about awkward moments. This is one, but the wise priest put a positive spin on a painful and seemingly negative incident. After Samuel answered his question, Eli said, "It is the LORD; let Him do what is good in His eyes" (1 Sam. 3:18). Wow! Imagine that; the wise encourager took the prophecy of his pending judgment like a champ. And he showed Samuel how he should behave even in the face of a divine rebuke.

These are the kinds of lessons that cannot be scripted. They last a lifetime. Eli taught young Samuel the value of honesty. And the prophetic boy fed it back to him when he least expected it.

Kids have incredible power when it comes to influencing adults. It doesn't take much to show them how to activate this power. In Sarah's case the teacher's simple lesson—do something small—released an unforgettable experience for Sarah and her entire church family. Samuel's value surfaced through the encouragement of an old priest. The perceived value was the common denominator in both cases—the biblical and the modern day.

Your children look to you for guidance about life and God. You don't need an advanced degree in child psychology to release the kid power within them. Just show them that they matter. They have value.

ACTION STEPS

Kid power is much needed nowadays. Your family will greatly benefit if you are able to unlock that additional power. Start from where you are and not where you hoped you'd be. Move in the right direction by taking the following action steps.

- Remember that God's throne room is open wide to all the subjects in His kingdom, even the little ones. Change your perspective by adopting one that says: kid power is real!

- Kid power is just as formidable as that of adults. On bended knees we share the same level of influence before the Almighty. Take time to pray with your children daily. Start the conversation with the question: What one thing would you like God to help you with? Then pray together about that issue.

- Before the end of the day locate a private space where you can offer this prayer:

Lord, help me to become a greater encourager to my children. I need Your wisdom to know how I can help them unlock kid power. I ask You this in the mighty name of Jesus. Amen.

Chapter 6

ADD FAITH TO
YOUR PRAYERS

———— ☼ ————

I RECENTLY TRAVELED TO Thailand with Compassion International. During some downtime from a heavy schedule of ministry we visited an elephant park where tourists could take elephant rides. I felt giddy; since my childhood this had been one of the items on my bucket list. The elephants were huge; each one had a tightly secured seat on its back that held two passengers. Although the size of a small sofa, the seat was dwarfed by the massive pachyderm. The driver sat bareback atop the elephant, in front of the passengers' seat.

I had to climb stairs about twelve feet in the air leading to a platform, with the elephant standing next to it. Then I gingerly maneuvered into the seat. Once I was seated, the operator secured a bar in front of me for safety. It was scary. But I took the thirty-minute ride, and my photos proved to my family that I actually rode on the back of an elephant.

After the ride ended, the elephant's handlers led him to the stable, where they placed one end of a rope—no more than two inches in diameter—around the beast's leg and staked the other end into the ground. This was not a metal rope, but one made of straw. Imagine that. A flimsy straw rope tethered a powerful animal to a wooden stake in the ground. The sight shocked me. Through my interpreter I asked the driver why the elephant would not pull up the stake or break the rope and wander off. The answer was just as shocking. The driver said the straw rope process had been used on the elephants since they were young. As calves the elephants didn't have the strength to escape, no matter how hard they pulled. Over time they began to believe they had no choice but to live with this restraint.

A male elephant is so certain of his captivity that even when he becomes fully grown, weighing upward of fifteen thousand pounds, he will not attempt to break free from the flimsy rope. I believe the same principle holds true for our children. If they learn the principle of mixing faith with their prayers, as adults they'll still pray that way. The Scriptures declare: "And the prayer of faith will save the sick, and the Lord will raise him up. And if he has committed any sins, he will be forgiven" (James 5:15).

According to James, God responds to faith. He is moved by faith. This is not a mystery. We don't have to search for some secret formula that gets God to respond to our prayers. We've been told: faith moves God!

In fact, the Bible teaches elsewhere: "And without faith it is impossible to please God, for he who comes to God must believe that He exists, and that He is a rewarder of those who diligently seek Him" (Heb. 11:6). Faith means to have a bold trust in God. Faith doesn't have to be gigantic or packaged in an adult-sized frame for it to be potent. Just as Jesus taught, it can be as small as a mustard seed and still move God (Matt. 17:20). A mustard seed is about the size of the tip of a ballpoint pen. That's tiny. Yet when it is mixed into our prayers, the result is huge. St. Augustine, a third-century theologian, said, "Faith is to believe what you do not see; the reward of this faith is to see what you believe."[1]

Be mindful of four things when you try to instill the role of faith and prayer in your child. Each is simple. But when they are packaged together, your child will be able to activate his kid power.

1. Faith comes from relationship.

2. Expectancy activates faith.

3. Faith requires focus.

4. Patience is a friend of faith.

Faith Comes From Relationship

You cannot have faith in God without a good relationship with Him. Although this sounds basic, many Christians ignore this truth. They want God's help, but they don't want to take time to build a strong relationship with Him. God wants relationship with you because, similar to you, He wants to be loved. Jesus taught: "'Love the Lord your God with all your heart and with all your soul and with all your strength and with all your mind;' and, 'Love your neighbor as yourself'" (Luke 10:27, NIV). This is the greatest commandment issued by God because it represents the greatest thing we can ever do—to love and serve the Lord. Faith is built on this premise!

Imagine that you and I were next-door neighbors, but whenever I saw you I seldom took the time to ask things such as: "How's your wife? How are the kids?" Or if we ran into each other at the neighborhood supermarket and I gave off body language that said, "I have no time to chat," yet then you saw me linger in the next aisle, talking to a total stranger.

How would you feel if after basically ignoring you on a daily basis I frequently asked to borrow your lawn mower or a cup of sugar? You'd would feel used and taken advantage of. Right?

That is how some of us interact with God; our entire relationship with Him is one-sided. Faith is *not* built on asking God for His help only when we need it. It's built on the trust we develop over a time-tested relationship. We need to spend time with God by reading the Bible, worshipping Him privately (and publicly), and even journaling our feelings and thoughts about Him. These actions help feed our relationship with the Lord.

By experience the psalmist David was able to write: "Delight yourself in the LORD, and He will give you the desires of your heart" (Ps. 37:4). When you are delighted with someone, you want to spend as much time with them as possible.

You can model this for your children by having a daily devotional time. When they ask you, "Why do you read your Bible every day and sing worship songs that we hear on Sundays?," tell them. They need to know that God wants you to talk to Him because you love Him and not just when you want something from Him. Frame the conversation in age-appropriate terms. Ask something like, "How would you feel if your friend Debbie only texted you when she wants to borrow something?"

Don't let the opportunity pass by. There are tons of ways to illustrate that faith grows from relationship. Use your own relationship with God as the source of the lesson. Your child knows you. They know your authenticity and sincerity. They have benefited from your honesty. Your words carry tremendous weight. Your child also knows some of your struggles and many of your needs. Explain how your relationship with God gives you confidence to approach Him with bold requests. Then talk about how He answered prayers in the past.

Don't ignore their real questions. For example, my daughters sometimes asked, "What happens when God doesn't answer one of your prayers? What do you do?" I would tell them, "I don't know why God didn't answer my prayer." Theologically this is called an appeal to mystery. But your kid doesn't care about that. What he does care about is this: "God thinks differently than I do. He has reasons that are too complicated for my small mind to fully understand. But since I love God so much, I'm not angry with Him. And since God loves me so much, I know that everything will work out for my best."

Your honesty will be refreshing. Years ago a feature in the *New Yorker* on billionaire Ted Turner reported that as a teenager Turner was religious. He even wanted to be a missionary. Then his younger sister became gravely ill. He was fifteen when Mary Jane, then twelve, contracted a form of lupus that attacks the body's tissues and immune system. Wracked with pain, she vomited constantly. Turner told the reporter that her screams filled the house. Ted regularly came home and held her hand, trying to comfort her. He prayed for her recovery; she prayed to die. After years of misery she passed, and Ted lost his faith. "I was taught that God was love and God was powerful," he said, "and I couldn't understand how someone so innocent should be made or allowed to suffer so."[2]

Turner's theology had holes. He wasn't taught what to do when our prayers are not answered. Don't let your kids fall victim to a loss of faith. They may never recover. Be honest. Honesty is the proof of a strong, emotionally healthy relationship.

A mother who worked from home prided herself on her professional image. One key to that image was her voice mail greeting, which was often a client's first contact with her. She said, "I worked on making it sound upbeat and enthusiastic, and thought I had succeeded until a friend left this message: 'Judy, this is Pam. I love your greeting, but do you know that you can hear your little boy in the background saying, 'Mommy, I gotta go potty'?"[3]

Be honest, even when honesty is embarrassing. This will prove invaluable to the spiritual formation of your child.

EXPECTANCY ACTIVATES FAITH

In his book, *Beyond Jabez*, Bruce Wilkinson shares the story of an old African woman who demonstrated faith in God's power to provide. Although she lived in a tiny mud hut, she had taken on 56 orphans.

A small group of Wilkinson's "Dream for Africa" volunteers had arrived in this grandmother's native Swaziland to plant gardens. On the final day of their visit, they came to her tiny home, surrounded by the many children in her care. A number of little gardens had been dug up all around the hut, but oddly, no plants were growing in any of them.

The volunteers learned that, earlier the same day, the woman told the children to dig lots of gardens. When the children asked her why—since they had neither seeds nor money—she responded, "Last night I asked God to send someone to plant gardens for us. We must be ready for them when they come."

Wilkinson's volunteers had come with hundreds of ready-to-plant seedlings. God sent them
to the very place where one of his servants had
begged for his intervening hand. The faithful
grandmother and her children were ready when
the answer came.[4]

The woman had taught her children that expectancy is
spelled F-A-I-T-H. Her faith in God moved her to take
action.

Having an expectation changes your behavior and
outlook. Take this example: One night Kari was baby-
sitting and had a terrible time getting the three kids
in her charge to bed. Their parents, who were out on
a date night, wanted them down by 8:00 p.m. It was
now seven forty-five, and not even the six-year-old was
listening; the girl was running around as if she was at
the park. The kids were a handful, to say the least. In a
moment of desperation the sitter said, "If you guys are in
bed and fall asleep by eight o'clock, your parents promised to give you a puppy tomorrow." Immediately they
all bolted to brush their teeth, put on pajamas, and dive
into bed. The moment their little heads hit their pillows,
they were fast asleep.

When the parents came home around 10:30 p.m., the
sitter walked to her car, thinking, "They'll sort it out in
the morning."

Expectation is a controlling force. Its command on
human behavior has even prompted scientific research.
Dr. Blair Justice, professor of psychology at the University

of Texas, writes: "What makes words so powerful that they can change molecular structures? The body and the mind are not separable. When we strongly believe that a pill, procedure or any other intervention into our problems will help us, most of us experience physiological changes known as a placebo response."[5]

If placebos have been shown to produce a positive response on the body, how much more will our positive expectations and faith in God? He believes in you. He believes in your children. In fact, God proudly proclaims: "'For I know the plans I have for you,' declares the LORD, 'plans to prosper you and not to harm you, plans to give you hope and a future'" (Jer. 29:11, NIV). God has plans for *your* children. These plans are positive and purposeful. As you share these truths with your little one, it will help bolster their confidence and expectation in God.

FAITH REQUIRES FOCUS

Since faith proclaims a bold trust in God, your child's allegiance must not be divided. Faith requires focus. As Hebrews 11:6 instructs, "He [God] is a rewarder of those who diligently seek Him." The earnest seekers after God are the diligent ones. They don't allow pain, discomfort, or even opportunities to pull them away from the matter at hand. Your child's prayer interest is where focus is required.

Do you really want it?

Before your child prays for something, help him focus by engaging in a conversation first. Ask: *"Do you really want God to do that?* If you do, then you *should* pray. I can even pray with you. If you're unsure, then let's *not* pray about it."* This kind of conversation helps your child determine their level of commitment to what they are seeking. True focus comes when there is a high and sustained interest. As a pastor I face the same circumstance with some of my adult members.

I remember, years ago, being approached by a woman requesting prayer. When I asked what she wanted God to do for her, she replied, "I want God to help me open my own car wash business." Before I agreed to pray with her, I asked, "Do you know how much it would take to open the type of car wash service that you have in mind?" Like a deer caught in the headlights, she stared at me and then muttered, "No, I don't." I replied, "Do a little research, and if you still want me to pray with you, I'll be glad to do so next week after service." I saw her the following week, and out of curiosity I followed up. Her response was, "The car wash I was thinking about is too expensive. I decided against it. Sorry. I don't need prayer anymore." We parted.

All too often people glibly pray about things without any real context or strong attachment to the fulfillment. Don't let your child fall into the trap of praying mindlessly. Help her probe her heart about the prayer request. Don't go overboard. Remember the objective here is not to interrogate or judge their desires—just to help your child understand that a real sense of focus has to accompany faith.

Kids are prone to distractions.

Children come with little minds and hearts that jump around from one area to another. You don't want to force them into adult-like behavior too soon. Your child deserves the freedom to be a child—albeit a responsible child. But a responsible child is still a child. Samuel the prophet was a responsible child, yet Eli had to coach him to stay focused and listen again for the voice of the Lord (1 Sam. 3:8–10). Similarly you need to coach your children through affirmation, loving forms of discipline, and teaching them the value of staying focused in the pursuit of their dreams. Focus is essential to faith-based prayer. This is the kind of prayers that secure answers and gain God's blessings.

Melissa Larsen works for the highly skilled K-9 Explosive Detection Unit of The Boeing Company. She trains dogs to detect explosives in order to maintain air travel safety. Some dogs can distinguish an estimated twenty thousand explosive compounds. When they find an explosive, they sit and stare. The fascinating thing is that quite a number of these dogs are rescue dogs that Melissa found in shelters. These shelters are filled with society's throwaways—dogs that landed there because they're difficult in some way. "You know there's plenty of hunting breeds out there that are discarded in the shelters, and it's usually because they are too active and too high strung and too obsessive, which is exactly what I like," Larsen said.

Larsen looks for dogs with a keen sense of smell and hunting instinct. These dogs are highly focused but still highly trainable. Her search begins as she walks through the kennels and casually bounces a tennis ball: "'What's this?' *Bounce, bounce, bounce*. 'Hey Buster, what's this?'" she says. "Most of the dogs show only cursory interest, but occasionally there is a pooch that becomes hyper-focused on the ball. That's a dog that gets a second look from Larsen. She gives the dog a good whiff of the tennis ball before taking it into an outside yard, where she's lodged the tennis ball into a chain link fence."

Larsen is looking for dogs consumed with the hunt to find the ball. They engage their powerful sense of smell and refuse to stop until they locate it. The selected dogs get enrolled into a ten-week training program to spot explosives and bombs. The program starts by introducing the dogs to the immense variety of explosive odors. "It's done by letting the dogs sniff a series of canisters. Only one has a small amount of explosive planted in it for purposes of the training. When the dog 'hits' on the correct can, it gets a reward. That reward is almost always a tennis ball. Soon the dog learns that finding a 'bomb' equals getting a ball." One rescue dog stared for over twenty minutes until he got his reward. This is real focus![6]

The value of focus in the activation of your child's faith is far more powerful. The reason why many of the first-century Christians were martyred was because they were God-focused. They worshipped Jesus as God, and they worshipped the infinite-personal God only. This was treason, because the Caesars would not tolerate this worshipping of only one God. Their worship became a special threat to the unity of the state during the third century and during the reign of Diocletian.[7] Helping develop a deep sense of focus in your children will embolden them in the faith. Focus is invaluable to every dimension of life, including our prayer life. The release of God's blessings, in response to their prayer of faith, is worth it.

PATIENCE IS A FRIEND OF FAITH

When former Arkansas senator David Pryor was a teenager, he worked as a congressional page. He loved the job so much he vowed to return someday as a member of Congress. To reinforce his vision, he hid a dime in a crack behind a statue in the Capitol, with the intention of retrieving it when he succeeded. Fifteen years later, as a newly elected member of the House of Representatives, he did just that. Pryor said this proves two things: one, that dreams in youth should never be underestimated; and two, that they don't clean the Capitol very much.[8] David Pryor was patient. He applied faith to see his dream come to pass. It took fifteen years, during which he grew through his teens, college, and more. Still, he modeled that patience is inseparable from faith.

Bring your life into divine alignment.

You've prayed in faith. Now what? How do you deal with the waiting period? I call those periods "divine delays." Your dream is in God's heart, but He's not allowing them to materialize right now. No one controls God or His timing. We can only control ourselves. During these times you must be patient. It takes time to learn patience. Since you control yourself, you can work to bring aspects of your life into alignment with God's moral standards.

Don't let impatience cause you to fall into a moral trap. A stained life will have major consequences. In 1999, when Ronald F. Thiemann, a Lutheran theologian, suddenly stepped down from his post as dean of the Harvard Divinity School, he said it was for "personal and professional reasons." *The Boston Globe* uncovered the real truth. They reported that he had been forced to resign after the school's IT department found thousands of pornographic images on his university-owned home computer. Dr. Thiemann had asked the IT guys to install a larger hard drive and to transfer the contents of the old drive to the new one.[9] Integrity matters! Blameless living is powerful! The lack of integrity causes delayed dreams to become derailed dreams. Sin affects your future! This is true even with children.

Divine alignment means you are not running ahead of God. And you are not behind Him. To live in obedience to God's laws, you walk side by side with Him. This honors God. You are also aligning your life with His standards. This is how you best position yourself for the blessings you've been praying and waiting for. When you help your kids understand these truths, it helps them to mature in a holistic way.

Maintain the right attitude.

Waiting on God is no excuse to walk around with a bad attitude. Teach your child to stay focused on the promises of God. It's OK to be discouraged, but it's not OK to let it soil your attitude. People will remember us for our attitude—good or bad. While you're hovering in this space of divine delays, keep your attitude pleasant, humble, and Christlike.

Again, you can't rush, pressure, or control God. You can only love Him while seeking to control yourself. Your love and obedience helps you avoid looking for ungodly or human shortcuts that only lead to pain and frustration.

Walk in assurance.

Even when faith is added to prayers, the possibility of divine delays is still inevitable. These delays help us to see the relationship between patience and faith. They are often inseparable friends. When I'm waiting on God, I'm constantly reminded of this point: God is the One who promised to bless me, and He has made plans for me.

Therefore I fill my mouth with praise, offering thanks to God because He knows what's best for me. Since there's nothing I can do, I learn to rest in His faithfulness. This is the assurance we have in Christ.

During an old broadcast of the popular radio program *Focus on the Family*, a special call-in episode aired on the National Day of Prayer. Listeners were invited to call in and share some of their stories of answered prayers. One caller shared:

> Hi, my name is Cathy and I'm calling from Green Bay, Wisconsin. I think some of the most exciting answers to prayer are the ones that our children witness. Once, while traveling with my two boys, we stopped to stretch our legs and when we came back to our car it wouldn't start. We were three hours from home and two hours from our destination and we didn't know a soul where we were.
>
> After trying to start the car several more times, I looked over at my oldest son, Tim, who was five at the time and I said, "We need to pray and ask God to make our car start." After we prayed, I looked at Tim and I said, "Well here we go." Would you believe the car started on the very first try. I wish you could have seen the look of surprise and wonder in my sons' face. Because of that object lesson from heaven, he will never forget that God really does hear and answer our prayers. Whether

for something very important or as simple as making a car start.[10]

It's the ordinary things of life that will help build our children's faith. I encourage you at times to pray with your children and even in front of them. Their faith will be buoyed as they see God's miracles unfold right before their eyes. When you pray, remember to pray in faith.

Faith is not about seeing or even having all of the answers surrounding the need. Faith is having an implicit trust in God's abilities. For example, one night a house caught fire and a young boy was forced to make his way to the roof. His dad stood on the ground below with outstretched arms, calling to him, "Son, jump! I'll catch you." He knew the boy had to jump to save his life. All the boy could see, however, was the flame, its smoke, and blackness. The boy was frozen was fear.

The thought of jumping from the roof was paralyzing. Yet his dad kept encouraging him to trust him and jump. His father kept yelling, "Jump! I will catch you." But the boy complained, "Daddy, I can't see you." The father replied, "But I can see you, and that's all that matters." The boy acted upon his trust of his dad and jumped into his arms. This is what God is asking you to teach your child to do. Jump into God's arms.

This story sums up the point: praying without faith is devoid of power. Without faith it is impossible to please God, and it is impossible to move God!

ACTION STEPS

Faith is such a remarkable gift from God. Use it often. As you grow in prayer, your faith in God is sure to grow. They are connected. Don't limit your prayer requests to small things. You ought to be bold when you come before the King. Let's rehearse some of our lessons from this chapter.

- Without faith you cannot please God.

- You cannot demonstrate faith in God without having a relationship with Him. You cannot have one without the other.

- Before you offer a prayer in faith, you must ask: Do I really want the blessing I'm about to pray for? After some thoughtful reflection and a genuine confidence to request the thing being sought, offer this prayer:

Almighty God, I've shied away before from making this request. But today I am pretty sure that I want to see this blessing all the way through. In Your goodness, I ask for You to bless me with _____. I ask You this in the name of Jesus. Amen.

Chapter 7

PRAYING GOD'S DREAM
FOR YOUR CHILD

---- ☼ ----

J ENNIFER KEMPTON BECAME a victim of sex trafficking. As reported by CNN.com, she saw and
experienced the worst of people. Yet she eventually
broke free from a life of sexual slavery and addiction.
Kempton was raped when she was twelve by a friend's
brother; that trauma was the start of her life's dark path.
Drugs became the only way she could deal with the pain.
Prostitution soon supported her drug habit.

Kempton spent more than five years on the streets,
enduring repeated beatings and sex with hundreds of
men. After a violent rape attack in 2013—the worst she'd
ever suffered—Kempton decided she had had enough of
life's hardships.

"She put a noose around her neck.... The rope broke,
and in that moment, she found a reason to live. 'God
came to me and spoke to me and he said I have a

purpose for you and it's not to die in the basement of a crack house,'" Kempton said.[1] This experience led to her becoming born again.

But four tattoos on her body were daily reminders of her life before Christ. "She had been branded by her former pimps. 'Branding' is when a pimp tattoos a woman with a mark to signify she is *his* property—like cattle."[2] One of the tattoos was over her groin area and read: "Property of Salem." Salem was the name of her pimp. Through the creative work of a gifted tattoo artist she was able to get the tattoos transformed. One now reads, in part, "1 Cor. 13." The fourth verse in 1 Corinthians 13 says: "Love is patient, love is kind. It does not envy, it does not boast, it is not proud" (NIV). God's redemptive love became her life verse.

Kempton later launched her own business named Survivor's Ink. She works with tattoo artists to redesign the tattoos that pimps branded on women formerly held captive in the sex trafficking industry.

Imagine hearing the voice of God while a rope is around your neck. God's voice was not condemning. He was letting her know that He had a dream for her. If God can have a dream for Jennifer, that means He has a dream for your child too. He has a dream for all of His creation and for all of our children.

If you are going to raise your children to pray, you must communicate to them over and over again: "God has a dream for you!" Remind them of the plans He expressed in Jeremiah 29:11: to prosper them and give them hope and a future. Whether they are young and innocent or have nicks and cuts to show their poor choices or their victimization, God still has a dream for them. That is a fact!

There are two things that must be done to see God's dream realized for your child. First, pray God's promises. Second, take courageous action in keeping with the will of God. Both are needed. One without the other will lead to disaster. Prayer alone will lead to the trap—one so many get caught in—that God is supposed to do it by Himself, apart from you. If you just take action without prayer, your action will be self-directed and devoid of divine guidance. This also leads to hopelessness and despair.

An old Scotsman operated a little rowboat for transporting passengers. One day a passenger noticed that on one oar the nice old man had carved the word "Prayer," and on the other oar the word "Action." Out of curiosity he asked what the carvings meant. The old man, a well-balanced Christian, glad for the opportunity to share his faith, said, "I will show you."

At that, he dropped one oar and plied the one called Action; the boat just went around in circles. Then he dropped that oar and began to ply the oar called Prayer, and the little boat just went around in circles again—this time in the other direction, but still in a circle going nowhere.

After this demonstration the old man picked up Prayer and Action. With both oars together, he sped swiftly over the water and explained to his passenger, "You see, that is the way it is in the Christian life. Dead works (or action) without prayer are useless, and prayer without action gets you nowhere. But prayer and action pulling together make for progress in and fulfilling God's dream for your life."

Let me show you how to use the two oars. Then you will be able to raise your children to do the same. This will help them to realize God's dream for their lives.

PRAY GOD'S PROMISES

God's promises are powerful! They are not bound by human limitations. They represent His vision of your future. They reflect His compassion and care for you. His promises are just as permanent and relevant as His laws and commandments. They never fade or become outdated.

His promises are just as dependable as His character. William Carey, the legendary missionary to India, said that "the future is as bright as the promises of God."[3] Matthew Henry, the great Bible scholar, once observed that God's promises "are to be our pleas in prayer."[4] This is why when you take hold of God's promises in prayer, you're really taking hold of God. His promises are His outstretched hand to you.

The promise fits your need.

Bible promises respond to the vast sea of humanity's needs. Help your child to find a promise that fits his circumstance and then use it as a prayer guide. The promise conveys what God did for another who faced a similar circumstance. It will boost your child's faith and confidence in God's ability. The promise also says what God can do when someone walks in obedience to His Word during times of difficulty.

If your child is facing a financial problem that you can't meet, a great promise is found in Philippians 4:19, which says: "And my God will meet all your needs according to the riches of his glory in Christ Jesus" (NIV). The way you can pray this verse is by unpacking the two assurances it offers:

1. "God will meet *my* needs"

2. "According to the glorious riches in Christ Jesus"

Your prayer can go something like this:

> *Dear God, my financial need is overwhelming, but I trust You. I ask that You work a miracle of provision for me and my family. Let this miracle bring glory to Your name. May people be brought closer to Jesus through this miracle! Use my need as a witnessing tool of Your great love and generosity. I pray this in the name of Jesus. Amen.*

If your child needs *insight and wisdom*, as they often do because of the rigor of school and jolting social pressures, then draw strength from this promise:

> Call to Me and I will answer you, and tell you [and even show you] great and mighty things, [things which have been confined and hidden], which you do not know and understand and cannot distinguish.
>
> —JEREMIAH 33:3, AMP

There are three assurances in this promise that shed light on how you can pray for wisdom and insight:

1. "Lord, open my eyes and mind that I may see and understand great and mighty things concerning my family, my school work, and how to better understand my teacher."

2. "Lord, help me to distinguish the confined and hidden things from my own thoughts. Give me the knowledge I need to make wise decisions, no matter their difficulty."

3. "God, You promised to answer me when I call to You. Grant me the sensitivity to hear Your voice and the courage to obey."

The promise is worth waiting for.

Some of God's promises come to pass quickly, while others may take a lifetime. Regardless of the gestation period, they are all worth waiting for. When Jesus told His disciples about the promised gift of the baptism of the Holy Spirit (Acts 1:3–5), they were told to wait in Jerusalem for the experience. They had no idea how long they were to wait, but they knew they did not want to miss what God had promised them. In ten days, on the Day of Pentecost, the promise was fulfilled. Even if the realization took longer than ten days, those disciples were so hungry for God's promises they would have waited forever. We need the same attitude with all of God's promises.

In *Heroes of the Holy Life* Wesley Duewel writes: "Give us a greater hunger, Lord, than we have ever known. Help us to wait in one accord until Your power is shown. Keep us, Your children, on our knees beseeching You with mighty pleas till floods of blessings like the seas sweep over all Your own."[5] To remain faithful as you wait, start memorizing Scripture. After a while you will find yourself confessing God's powerful promises in the face of trials.

These promises will become a part of your life. They will force you to adopt the practice of Charles Spurgeon, who once said that he never left behind a promise until he received it, simply meditating on it until its fruit fell into his hand. Spurgeon was envisioning the beauty and blessing inherent with the promise. He could not see himself living without it. God promised it to him! He could not leave it alone. You must reach the same conclusion. Fight for the promise. God promised you this blessing! Martin Luther, the great reformer, took a similar approach. He said when he got ahold of a promise, he looked at it like a fruit tree, shaking it until the fruit fell.

These spiritual champions were ordinary people like you and me. What made them leave a mark on history is that they dared to believe God. They defeated doubt by facing it head on. You can do the same!

TAKE COURAGEOUS ACTION

When you pray God's promises, you must also *take courageous action*. You cannot give in to the notion: "If God wants it to happen, it will happen. If it's meant to be, it will be." This kind of fatalistic thinking thwarts faith and real progress. Even intercessors sometimes fall back on that numbing kind of reasoning. They pray and pray but never take action.

David didn't operate this way when he learned that God had a dream for him. When David was a teenager, Samuel, the revered prophet, prophesied that David, not Saul (the present king), would be king of Israel. The prophecy was God's way of letting David know He had a dream for him (1 Sam. 16:11–13). Who would have thought that the son of a shepherd would become the king of a nation? Only God.

Seize God-opportunities.

Pray all you want, but there was no way Samuel's prophecy over David was going to come about without some type of major undertaking in the natural. There had to be God-opportunities that David seized. When he took hold of them, they became stepping-stones that led to realizing God's dream. That is exactly what happened. Young David seized the God-opportunities that came his way.

The first big one came in the middle of an ordinary errand. His dad asked him to deliver a care package to his three older brothers, soldiers in Saul's army (1 Sam. 17:12–19). They were fighting the Philistines. To David's surprise, when he arrived where the army was stationed, the soldiers were just hanging around. No one was fighting. That's because Goliath, a nine-foot-plus tall Philistine, was offering a challenge that no one wanted to take on (1 Sam. 17:4–11). For forty consecutive days he issued a simple proposition to the Israelite army. Let me condense it for you. Goliath shouted, "If one of your guys kills me, our nation will be your slaves. But if I kill your fighter, the Jews will become our slaves."

With one glimpse of his massive strength the soldiers recoiled in fear. David chose to rise to the occasion. This popular Bible account shows that David killed Goliath with his slingshot. The backstory, however, shows how God-opportunities work. The thousands of Jewish soldiers couldn't see a God-opportunity. They were paralyzed by Goliath's size. Not David. He was naturally inquisitive.

He asked all of the right questions about Goliath, including one about Saul's offer to give tax-free living to the soldier who defeated Goliath. David had always been a nosey kid. This was his natural bent. He was also naturally brave and protective. He had the heart of a warrior. He was hardwired to kill a bear and a lion, having eliminated these two vicious animals when they tried to eat through his flock. He planned the same approach with Goliath. David seized this God-opportunity by following his heart.

You must do the same. This is shown by a story about a young man who wished to marry the farmer's beautiful daughter. He went to the farmer to ask for her hand:

> The farmer looked him over and said, "Son, go stand out in that field. I'm going to release three bulls, one at a time. If you can catch the tail of any one of the three bulls, you can marry my daughter."
>
> The barn door opened and out ran the biggest, meanest-looking bull he had ever seen. He decided that one of the next bulls had to be a better choice than this one, so he ran over to the side and let the bull pass through the pasture out the back gate.
>
> The barn door opened again. Unbelievable. He had never seen anything so big and fierce in his life. It stood pawing the ground, grunting, slinging slobber as it eyed him. Whatever the next bull was like, it had to be a better choice than this one. He ran to the fence and let the bull pass through the pasture, out the back gate.
>
> The door opened a third time. A smile came across his face. This was the weakest, scrawniest little bull he had ever seen. This one was his bull. As the bull came running by, he positioned himself

just right and jumped at just the exact moment.
He grabbed…but the bull had not tail![6]

Life is full of opportunities. If you wait around for
what seems to be the perfect one, you may miss out
altogether.

God-opportunities are all around you. They may show
up with a label that reads "problem." Similar to David,
when you defeat the problem, you gain the reputation of
being a giant-killer. Don't wait to solve the large problems so that everyone can take note of your victory. First
kill the bear or lion in front of you. This will prepare
you for the larger problem—the Goliaths that will enter
your life. You must defeat them before you can sit on the
throne.

Make divine connections.

God ingeniously places people in our path to help us
collaborate, form strategic partnerships, and learn the
lessons vital to fulfilling His dreams for our lives. We
see that David had three types of relationships that were
key to his realization of God's dream for him. Remember,
God wanted David to become king. Prayer alone was not
going to be the answer. Bold acts on David's part were
critical pieces of the puzzle. It is one thing to kill a giant,
but it takes another type of courage to make meaningful
relationships. David had a confidant, coach, and confronter. They each played a pivotal role in his development and the shaping of his persona.

David's confidant

Saul's son Jonathan was David's confidant (1 Sam. 18:1–4). Jonathan, a prince in Israel, took a real liking to David once he saw how he handled himself against Goliath. The young men became lifelong friends. With a confidant you're not afraid to share your secrets, pain, aspirations, and longings—and they with you. The relationship is mutually vulnerable.

As David's confidant Jonathan helped him see his natural gift of influence. You need a royal demeanor to become king. David was a shepherd. He knew nothing of royalty, nor the protocol that comes with it. Jonathan was a prince. Regal carriage was all he knew. This was a divine connection. Jonathan had what David needed. In the providence of God, He caused them to meet and forge a deep friendship—one that eventually helped David become what God called him to be.

Your child will need a confidant. This is someone beyond the home. You can begin praying for that person to surface at the appropriate time. A confidant is a friend—a really good friend. This is someone apart from a spouse. This is a peer with whom your child will feel extremely comfortable. God will use this person to deposit some key things within your child. These things will come in handy as he pursues God's dream for his life.

David's coach

David also needed a coach to help him advance toward God's dream for his life. Samuel the prophet played that role. Coaches know how to pull the best out of you. They challenge you to step up and to get to the next level. They never let you settle for mediocrity. Samuel saw big leadership gifts in David and encouraged him to develop them.

Mark Twain said: "Keep away from people who try to belittle your ambitions. Small people always do that, but the really great make you feel that you too can become great."[7] A coach will not tear you down, but he will build you up. Your child's coach can be a much older sibling, a grandparent, a teacher, or a friend of the family. Coaches mentor her for her destiny. They provide personalized guidance through life's transitions. A coach provides insight to nagging questions, which—left unanswered—can impede your child's growth. Once answered, the ceiling is removed. Growth occurs.

When Saul attempted to kill young David out of jealousy, David went to find comfort and wisdom in Samuel (1 Sam. 19:18). Samuel was able to provide David with the needed perspective so that God's dream of his becoming king would not be aborted. David learned how to pray, cast his cares on the Lord, and walk in faith because of Samuel. He also learned how to integrate spirituality as part of his leadership traits when involved in leading arms of government. This is a hard feat. Many people are good in secular roles but exhibit a shallow spiritual life. Others have a strong spiritual life but demonstrate ineffective leadership when engaged in the broader society. David excelled at both, largely due to Samuel's coaching.

Samuel believed in David. This made all the difference in the world. A coach's enthusiastic support of you goes way beyond the affirmation of your skills. It lifts your spirit and buoys your faith, especially when fiery trials don't seem to let up. Because the coach believes in you, you find the confidence to also believe in yourself.

Bill Schuffenhauer is an American bobsledder who has competed in three Winter Olympics and was the silver medal winner in the four-man event in Salt Lake City in 2002. Thanks to the publicity surrounding Olympic athletes, the world soon learned a lot about this man:

> His parents were drug addicts...his mother was a prostitute who was often beaten in front of him....He stole from people; he ate from garbage cans; he got locked up in juvenile detention for breaking into a bike shop when he was trying to get something he could sell for money so he could eat.
>
> His mom and stepfather were constantly getting evicted. When he wasn't homeless and living in a park, he lived in foster homes. He skipped school a lot. He drank and got high on weed....Just around the time he was entering junior high, Schuffenhauer's maternal grandmother, Sadie Muniz, took him in. She lived in the town of Roy, Utah, about thirty minutes north of Salt Lake City.[8]

He tearfully talked to reporters about her steadying influence and how she was always there to pull him up or pull him back when he started messing up again. He told of how she reminded him to "never give up and always push on" in life.[9] Because she never gave up on him, he began to go to school regularly and turn his life around. He's now a famed Olympian. Schuffenhauer's maternal grandmother coached him in the affairs of life. She saw God's dream for him, and through her guidance he was able to realize it.

Pray that God brings coaches into your child's life who believe in him when he may not believe in himself. Success in life takes prayer and courageous action.

David's confronter

A confronter is also a godsend. No one wants a confronter, but God knows we need them. Your dream is not simply yours alone. It was first God's. In fact, your prayers and those of your children have been for God's dream to come to pass. For that to occur, a confronter is instrumental to your destiny, and your children's.

Joab was David's confronter. He was also a military man—a fierce warrior who came into David's life in response to a challenge. David had just become king of Israel, but his rule had yet to be fully secured. Jerusalem, formerly known as Jebus, remained to be conquered. David barked out an order: "'Whoever strikes Jebus first will be the commander and leader of the army,' so Joab, the son of Zeruiah, went up first and became the commander" (1 Chron. 11:6).

He defeated the Jebusites, and Jerusalem became known as the City of David. It's also where David established his residence and headquarters. Through this victory Joab became David's general. Over the years of his tenure as general Joab won many other military campaigns and conquered formidable cities for the sake of David. However, over time, he grew to become David's confronter.

Divine confronters are talented people. They come into your life through many avenues and at different junctures. The funny thing about them is that they don't need you to be successful. They are very talented in their own right. Such was the case with Joab. We learn early on that: "He [David] fortified the city [Jerusalem] all around from the Millo encircling the stronghold, while Joab preserved the rest of the city" (1 Chron. 11:8). Imagine that. David built up half of Jerusalem, and Joab restored the other half of the city that would later become known as *the Holy City*. Joab was a significant leader.

A confronter may challenge your beliefs and values. If you keep your cool, however, knowing that God allows divine connections into your life for a reason, you'll reap a huge benefit from the confrontation. You'll become clearer in your views, stronger in your ability to speak convincingly, and better positioned to influence others.

Often praying people don't recognize the role of confronters in their lives. We try to pray them away, thinking they are the planting of Satan. There may come a time that your confronter must be extricated from your life, but you must be discerning so that God's dream is not disrupted or aborted.

A confronter may challenge your character and personal style, but that is for your good. You will become stronger and more competent in leading a diverse team. You will have fewer character defects and more socially acceptable habits. A confronter may even challenge your goals and motivation. As a result you will become more focused, relevant, and accomplished. You will abandon unnecessary goals to arrive at a purer motivation.

If adults have a tough time juggling these critical relationships, you have to be really intentional as a parent to help your little one navigate them. God uses relationships, just as He will use all of life to complete our spiritual formation. Your children must learn how to pray through relationship dynamics, or else they'll jump from one school to the next. They'll find a reason to move from one team to the next, or from one relationship to the next, in search of perfection.

A little seven-year-old in our children's church approached a teacher with this prayer request: "Can you pray with me that God gives me a new daddy?"

The wise teacher asked, "What's wrong with the one you have?"

"I don't like him! He's always correcting me," Brittany shared.

Now, there may be some truth to the need for that dad to change his parenting style. But the teacher said, "Sweetheart, you can't choose who your father is. Can we pray that God helps you to learn how to be a better daughter and your dad to be a nicer daddy?" She nodded her head up and down in agreement with the new direction of prayer.

Biblical truths help shape our prayers and our attitude toward prayer. Keep your children's prayers centered in Scripture, and God's dream for them will be sure to come to pass.

ACTION STEPS

Your children are so important to God that He actually has a dream for their life and future. Your prayers, and theirs, must align with that dream. Discovering this dream takes time. But commit to having fun in the discovery process. Let's review a few things.

- God's dream for your child will naturally fit his gifts, skill set, and personality.

- There are two things you must do to realize God's dream for your life and that of your children—pray God's promises and take courageous action.

Establish a special moment this week to ask your child this question: What do you think God's dream is for your life? After you talk for a while, find a couple of main points in his answer that you can pray with him about. Pray:

> *Loving God, I thank You because You have a dream for my child. I ask that You would give him wisdom and courage throughout his life to make the right decisions so that Your dream comes to pass. I ask You this in the mighty name of Jesus. Amen.*

Chapter 8

HELP, GOD!

———— ☼ ————

H ELP, GOD!" THIS little prayer rescued me many times when my children were growing up. When I didn't know how to pray, the words "Help, God!" just popped out repeatedly. If you've never uttered this plea, try it. It is my gift to you.

As I write this chapter, two families I know are praying this prayer because their kids are acting up. In one family the eight-year-old is cutting herself as a way of coping with her parents' divorce. Melanie is very close to her dad, and the thought of seeing him only every other weekend weighs heavily on her little heart. Both parents are Christ-followers, but the strain of money problems and a lack of proper boundaries led to the demise of their marriage. Yet both parents are wholly committed to the ongoing spiritual formation of Melanie and her two older siblings.

The other household is grappling with a thirteen-year-old whose attitude has become very ugly. Kevin used to love praying with the family, participating in youth group, and reading his Bible. Not only has he stopped those activities, but also he claims he no longer believes in God. The mere mention of the word *church* causes a big fight. The father is a strong Christian, while Kevin's mother is relatively new in her walk with the Lord. She has been practicing her faith for about three years and is quite eager to grow. They both want Kevin to return to Christ and resume his spiritual development.

Both families have it rough right now. Even with counseling, there are no easy answers. Each set of parents is committed to helping their children learn prayer and other vital spiritual disciplines.

However, it's a delicate dance. If these parents push too hard, they will lose them. If they're too "hands off," their kids' bad habits could worsen. Kids are not robots that we can program. I sometimes wish they were. God, in His infinite wisdom, designed them to be far more intricate creatures than that. To parent your child effectively during turbulent times, you must join the chorus of intercessors with the two-word prayer that often helped me.

This simple prayer taught me two lessons that shaped the spiritual side of my parenting. It reminded me that I must always focus on helping my kids build *good habits* and a *great heart*. No matter what the child's stage of development or ugly attitude, my discouraged state of mind, or some unforeseen problem, I kept my parental eye on these two things—building good habits and building a great heart.

Build Good Habits

Your child's spiritual formation will come from good habits that are grounded in the Bible. Children need a spiritual reality that provides them plausible answers to five critical questions:

1. Does God exist? What is He like?

2. How was the world created and formed?

3. What is my purpose and that of humanity?

4. Is there life after death?

5. What is true? How do I live in light of that truth?

Whether your children articulate these questions or not, they are on their hearts and minds. Without solid answers they won't have anchors to draw closer to the Lord. When my daughter Jessica was about five years old, she asked me, "Dad, do caterpillars yawn?" We were driving to the mall, and Jess wanted this question answered. Truthfully I had never thought about this, and frankly I didn't care. But she did. She was really asking, "How was the world created?" I answered, "Sweetheart, I really don't know if caterpillars yawn." I meant to look it up, but to this day I've still never gotten around to it. But I did answer the question *behind* her question numerous times. She was satisfied with my answer that God created the world. But children grow, and our answers must grow with them, fitting their present maturity level.

Learn the answers.

If your child is misbehaving and disrupting the family, don't rush to a quick judgment. The real issue may be their need for an answer to one of the five basic questions. In the spiritual formation of your children the goal is to help them trust their religious practices in spite of challenges that will come against their faith. That's why the Bible encourages parents to *"train up* a child in the way he should go, and when he is old he will not depart from it"* (Prov. 22:6, emphasis added).

Try to learn what your child's needs are. Just as a doctor performs various tests on her patient before offering a prognosis, you must do the same. You do this by spending time together. Good parents know they are not their child's friend. If this line has become blurred in your household, ask the Lord to give you wisdom to reestablish healthy parental boundaries.

If you need help answering the five questions that help your child develop a healthy spiritual life, look to your church. If you don't have a home church, make finding one a top priority. Your child needs to learn good habits, not simply through conversation but also by what you model. When you become a part of a local church, that community of Christ-followers should provide a wealth of guidance in spiritual things. Your Bible knowledge is sure to grow. Whatever gaps exist on the local church level can be filled with books, websites, and other resources.

Good habits come easier when you are a part of a community that models those habits. The habits of prayer, Bible study, and connecting with other Christians who are excited about their devotion to Christ will have a positive impact on your life. This in turn will affect your children. A church that supports parents in the process of raising godly kids will prove invaluable.

Sometimes simply providing answers is not enough. You have to give your child space to process the answers. Nine-year-old Jonathan needed some space and time to make a decision. This is what he said to his parents, Doris and Javier, after a class on water baptism. Their church offered a two-week water baptism class for kids. At the end most kids rushed to sign up, but not Jonathan. He opted out. His parents didn't know how to broach the topic with their little guy. "What was he thinking? Where was he confused about his relationship with Christ?" they were thinking. Although these questions troubled them, they waited to see if Jonathan would bring up the topic. In a few days he shared, "Water baptism is a big decision, and I have to pray about it first."

Several months passed, and kids' baptism enrollment came up again. This time Jonathan eagerly said, "I want Jesus to be my Savior. I want to be a Christian!" His parents prayed with him, and Jonathan cried as he felt the presence of God envelop him. After this brief prayer time he exclaimed, "I just feel so happy! I'm happy. I'm a Christian." When water baptism rolled around, it had all the more meaning to Jonathan because it was *his* decision.

Focus on the habit.

Bad behavior can be a huge distraction. To stay motivated as you build your child's spiritual life, you need fuel. This means your life cannot be consumed by your child's. This is a very common and serious mistake many parents make. You have to create space and time for your own personal devotions and activities. Maintain a balanced life. These habits will help fill your emotional bank account. This will give you the needed energy and clarity of mind to be effective tackling problems that surface in the home.

When your child grows resentful of spiritual habits you're trying to foster, take a step back and pray. Don't panic. Win the battle on your knees! You cannot force the issue. It must happen willingly if it's going to stick. If your child doesn't want to pray, focus on their moral character. For example, encourage them to join a debate club where the students tackle heavy issues. Have videos lying around the house that feature Christian apologists who tackle heavy subjects such as social justice, war, or Islam versus Christianity.

The point is this: spiritual development is not a one-track process. If your child is going through a funky period where he is not open to attending youth groups at church, look for ways to expose him to Christian athletes or some of the nontraditional ministries. This is where a mission trip, domestic or overseas, may prove eye-opening and positive. After some of our teens participated in a mission trip to Haiti and Nicaragua, their lives took a turn for the better. In prayer ask God to give you creative ideas that will help stimulate spiritual growth in your child. Every child is different. What works for one may not work for the other.

Focus on good habits.

Spiritual habits are not the only habits that you want to cultivate. A natural habit can sometimes trigger a thirst for a spiritual one. Natural habits come from a set of house rules. Expectations will shape a child's behavior toward others. For example, if you want your child to clear the table when she has finished eating, establish the rule. And reinforce it. Don't be afraid of your child. If you want your child to have a proper diet, buy and cook the meals that will help reinforce that expectation.

Permissive parents harm their children's future by giving them the impression that anything goes. Billy Graham once said, "A child who is allowed to be disrespectful to his parents will not have respect for anyone."[1] The parents' job is to outline the expectations for the children living under their roof. Children need stable authority.

Establish boundaries for your children. Boundaries help your child to answer the questions: What is expected of me? How should I act? Your boundaries should be designed to help your child mature and learn how to take on age-appropriate responsibilities. Don't bail her out of every mess she gets into. She must learn the consequences of her actions even when the consequences are grave. Even when your children become adults, you must maintain this sensitivity to boundaries. You cannot keep investing resources to improve your adult child's quality of life. Boundaries help them stand on their own two feet—spiritually, emotionally, and financially.

Model the preferred habit.

We all know children are impressionable. You are a powerful role model, even nonverbally. Peter proved this when he urged believing wives to "be submissive to your own husbands, so that if any do not obey the word, they may be won without a word by the conduct of their wives, as they see the purity and reverence of your lives" (1 Pet. 3:1–2). If unbelieving husbands can be influenced and shaped by their believing wives, how much more can impressionable children? Let your kids see the habits at work in your life that you want developed in theirs.

Your loving actions will be undeniable and ultimately irresistible. Let your love be practical. Show a genuine interest in their hobbies and interests. Connect your kids with you by involving them with some of your interests, hobbies, and activities. They will learn who you are, what you love, and what you're becoming when they connect with you. Your Christlikeness, coupled with your powerful prayers, will win them over.

BUILD GREAT HEART

> The devil, according to legend, once advertised his tools for sale at a public auction. When the prospective buyers assembled, there was one oddly shaped tool which was labeled, "Not for sale." Asked to explain why this was, the devil answered, "I can spare my other tools, but I cannot spare this one. It is the most useful implement that I have. It is called discouragement, and with it I can work my way into hearts otherwise inaccessible. When I get this tool into a man's heart, the way is open to plant anything there I desire."[2]

How true! This is why I'm convinced that a big part of raising good kids is helping them build great hearts. Too many people get easily sidelined by discouragement. They lack passion, drive, and the heart to become spiritual champions. If you help your children build a heart of passion for service and missional living, there will be no room for discouragement to lodge in their souls.

In his book *Living a Life of Fire* the legendary international evangelist Reinhard Bonnke shares the story about his call to preach the gospel in Africa when he was just a young child growing up in Germany. Young Reinhard ran to his dad, a pastor, and said: "'Father, Father, God spoke to me in church today and said I must preach the gospel in Africa!' I must have appeared to him like a bouncing puppy yapping out my excitement.... Then he looked at me with a puzzled and somber expression. 'Your brother Martin will be my heir, Reinhard. He will be the preacher of the gospel in this family.'"[3]

Reinhard then gives us a glimpse of what happened in his heart. He writes: "Disappointment darkened my heart. His [my father's] tone of voice spoke louder than his words. It told me he was in deep doubt about my claim.... On this day I began to understand that I had two fathers. An earthly father and a heavenly Father. Until that moment, I had assumed they spoke with one voice."[4] Fortunately Reinhard never allowed discouragement to stunt his growth. His big heart for the souls of the African people led him to conduct crusades that drew more than a million people at a time. He's brought millions of people to a saving knowledge of Jesus Christ in Africa and around the world. One reason behind his phenomenal success is his perspective: he maintains a great heart for God!

Pain is not the end of life.

> Dr. Park Tucker, former chaplain of the federal penitentiary in Atlanta, Georgia, told of walking down the street in a certain city, feeling low and depressed and worried about life in general. As he walked along, he lifted his eyes for a moment to the window of a funeral home across the street. He blinked his eyes a couple of times, wondering whether his eyes were deceiving him.

But sure enough…in the window of that funeral home was this sign…"Why walk around half-dead? We can bury you for $69.50. P.S. We also give green stamps." Dr. Tucker said the humor of it was good medicine for his soul. Many people are walking around half-dead because worry has built a mountain of problems over which they believe there is no path. They have surrendered to fate.[5]

Have you trained your child to handle pain? I am referring to disappointment—the pain of the soul. This training is very much a part of children's spiritual formation. Life is not like the movies. Everything doesn't work out perfectly in the beginning, middle, or end all the time. It doesn't mean you didn't exercise faith or fail to offer enough prayer. Without a sound theology on pain we are left to handle problems as the rest of the world does. You cannot raise your kids to be defenseless and ill-equipped to face life's problems.

In 2015 I started writing op-ed pieces for secular national media outlets. My aim was to offer solutions to combat the dearth of critical thinking in the broader culture on matters of faith, family, and life. In one article I offered an alternate perspective to the pain of widespread tragedies, such as the 2015 suicide bombing that caused the death of approximately 130 people in Paris. When these kinds of tragedies strike, many people, secular and Christian alike, ask, "God, why?" I shared that this question is the wrong one because "it's too incriminating against God and too numbing to the sufferer. Better, we should ask: 'God, now what?'"[6] Admittedly, evil is very complex. So we must have a well-informed theology so that we don't lose hope or heart.

Joyce Meyer painfully shared how her father's inability to function as a father created unimaginable pain: "I had lots of hurt and lots of pain, lots of woundedness, bruises, broken heartedness in my life. I was abused sexually by my father, abused mentally, emotionally. My mom didn't know what to do about it, and she was being hurt in the process. So she just didn't deal with it. And I can guarantee you, just because you don't deal with something, that doesn't make it go away."[7]

Spiritual formation must include helping your kids to build great hearts. This way they can combat natural and spiritual forces bent on wiping them out through discouragement.

Failure is not the end of life.

My cousin Stewart and I are the same age. When we were both in seventh grade, I was placed in a gifted class. Even then, as a lover of learning and high educational achievement, I was immensely proud of my special ranking. I landed in the second highest of the four gifted classes. Those of us in these classes not only had bragging rights, but we also had the privilege of skipping eighth grade.

In the standard seventh grade classes, students were ranked from 7-1 down to 7-21. This was a huge middle school. Stewart had the double misfortune of being placed in class 7-15 and of being my cousin. I teased him mercilessly. Whenever he'd come into a room, I'd look at my watch and announce that it was seven fifteen no matter what time of day it was. And I'd do anything to work in a seven fifteen dig to bug Stewart. My constant deriding grated on his nerves and self-esteem so badly that Stewart began to work hard at applying himself in school.

Today he is an executive in a telecommunications company and has completed his doctoral studies at a top engineering school. The other day he admitted to me that whenever he hears seven fifteen, he still winces a little and then chuckles. Recently he was in the airport on a business trip and he heard the announcement over the intercom, "This is the last call for flight 715." At this, all my childhood digs came rushing back to Stewart's memory, and he laughed to himself as he walked to his terminal. He has since told me that my teasing made him feel like a loser back then. But even in the face of browbeating defeat, Stewart turned his failure into success.[8] This is because he had built the great heart of a champion. Failure was not powerful enough to pin his shoulders to the mat, as winning wrestlers do to their opponents in the ring.

To help your kids overcome the fear of failure, help them keep their eyes on the main objective—not small setbacks. Disappointment and failure can eat away at your child's soul and self-worth. That is what your lessons must focus on combatting. To protect your children's sense of self-worth, let them know that failure does not diminish their value. There is a difference between what you fail to accomplish and who you are. The former speaks of function and action while the latter represents a powerful human being who has the ability to create and reorder his steps. Failure is the outcome of an event but not a descriptor of the person behind the event.

Pamela and her husband, Richie, taught their son Robby to have heart. For his tenth birthday they gave him a black Labrador retriever. They wanted Robby to learn how to be responsible. So they told him he had to take care of the dog. Robby named him Ben; the dog was his best friend in life. Robby had him for about ten months, and then, the following summer, they went for a bike ride. Afterward Robby went inside the house and forgot to tie up Ben, who was lying down under a shade tree. This was not the first time.

The dog ran off. This was not the first time that had happened either. The family went looking for him, but they never found him. Robby was down on himself for his failure to tie up Ben. But he never gave up the search, even months later. Then one Tuesday morning, exactly ten months after Ben had vanished, Robby was doing the dishes. He just happened to look out the window, and there was Ben, sitting and looking through the window at Robby. So Ben is back now, and Robby is thrilled. He said he prayed every day for his friend to return home. He said the last time he prayed was the night before Ben came home. For ten months he never stopped praying.

Getting knocked down by life is common. Getting up is uncommon. Teach your kids to keep getting up. This will help them throughout every stage of life, where they may meet up with pain and failure.

> The man in the supermarket was pushing a cart which contained, among other things, a screaming baby. As the man proceeded along the aisles, he kept repeating softly, "Keep calm, George. Don't get excited, George. Don't get excited, George. Don't yell, George."
>
> An elderly lady watching with admiration said to the man, "You are certainly to be commended for your patience in trying to quiet little George."
>
> "Lady," he declared, "I'm George."[9]

Children can sometimes have a tough time. Family structures are often more complicated than they used to be. Children are exposed to a plethora of sexual and commercial messages on a daily basis. Social media and other technological advances drastically change childhood dynamics. We must be sympathetic with them. In the same breath we parents need sympathy too.

Noted child psychologist and author Dr. James Dobson answers the troubling question many parents ask: "What is the biggest obstacle facing the family right now? It is over-commitment; time pressure. There is nothing that will destroy family life more insidiously than hectic schedules and busy lives, where spouses are too exhausted to communicate, too worn out to have sex, too fatigued to talk to the kids. That frantic lifestyle is just as destructive as one involving outbroken sin. If Satan can't make you sin, he'll make you busy, and that's just about the same thing."[10] This problem of overscheduling can be easily remedied by being more thoughtful about your priorities.

But the next time you're on your knees crying out, "Help, God!," because your kid has done another thoughtless thing, remember to stay focused. True success is helping them to build good habits and a great heart.

Action Steps

Parenting needs sober judgment. Don't be afraid to surrender to the reality that you just don't know how to pray in every given situation. Little prayers pack a lot of spiritual power. Don't be afraid of building your prayer vocabulary with them. God looks at the heart more than He does the words.

- Keep your focus simple and clear so you keep child-rearing problems in proper perspective.

- If your child has lost sight of or is unwilling to work on spiritual formation issues, ask what other developmental area you can build up.

- When it's time to sing the two-word song
  of the intercessors, "Help, God!," find
  a quiet space where this prayer can be
  offered. Then go for it! Belt it out! God will
  understand all of the unspoken words of
  your heart.

Chapter 9

GOD, ARE YOU OK?

———— ☀ ————

Go D, ARE YOU OK?" four-year-old Vinnie prayed. "That's an unusual prayer," his mother commented as she pulled the blanket under his chin. "I was just curious," he said, "because you said that God will speak to my heart when I pray. I've never heard Him say anything. So I was wondering if He was OK." Phyllis paused to think of the best way to answer her son's tough question. Before she could figure out where to begin, Vinnie said, "Can we have pancakes for breakfast in the morning?" Then he turned over and faced his little teddy bear, the signal that he was ready to sleep.

A cartoon pictured a little boy kneeling in prayer. Obviously disgruntled with God, he was saying, "Aunt Harriet hasn't gotten married, Uncle Hubert hasn't any work, and Daddy's hair is still falling out. I'm getting tired of praying for this family without getting any results."[1]

Although these illustrations are comedic, at some point you will have to answer some of your child's troublesome questions about God. Like most parents you hope the question is soon forgotten, as in the case of Phyllis. But what happens when it's not? It can become a stumbling block to your little one's spiritual progress. Children are curious about God. They want to know what He's like and who He really is. And they deserve a good answer.

One of the teachers in our children's church finds herself each year having to teach the kids that God's not an old man. They automatically envision Him as such because He has existed forever and Jesus came more than two thousand years ago. To counter the notion, she tells them to think of God as one of their friends— the nice friend and not the mean one. The mean friend makes fun of you if you fall down; the nice one runs to check if you're OK. The latter is the type of God we pray to and serve.

GOD IS OK

The answer to Vinnie's question, "God, are You OK?" is a resounding "Yes!" God is all sufficient! He has no needs. God is OK! What Vinnie was trying to get at is this: Why does God sometime respond to my prayers immediately and other times not respond at all? Jesus spoke to that very point when He told His disciples that "they should always pray and not give up" (Luke 18:1,

NIV). Persistence in prayer is a quality we all need if our prayer lives are to blossom into something special.

Being persistent is not being a nuisance. D. L. Moody drew that same perspective when he said: "Some people think God does not like to be troubled with our constant coming and asking. The way to trouble God is not to come at all."[2]

In the garden of Gethsemane Jesus prayed for the same thing three times over what appears to be a three-hour time span (Matt. 26:44). Three times He prayed: "My Father, if it is not possible for this cup to be taken away unless I drink it, may your will be done" (Matt. 26:42, NIV). His persistence was borne out of a troubled heart. He was never doubtful or unsure of God's willingness to answer Him.

Jesus was just gripped by the thought of being alienated from God. Never before was this a reality. The thought of bearing the sins of the world as He hung from the forthcoming cross weighed heavily on His heart. His persistence in prayer was simply a confirmation that the cross was the only option. His persistence, like yours, bore the fruit of courage. The cross had to occur. God's redemptive love had to be demonstrated through His atoning death, burial, and resurrection. God's silence confirmed the necessity of Jesus's impending death. God was OK! Humanity was about to have a Savior. All was well! Jesus's courageous act was a by-product of His persistence in prayer. God's silence satisfied Jesus's prayer request. The cross was God's will—and Jesus's too. All was well!

The Bible shows that Paul, the great apostle, also prayed three times concerning one of his personal needs. The time span for his prayers is unknown. But what is known is the answer. Paul said: "I asked the Lord three times that this thing [a thorn in the flesh] might depart from me. But He said to me, 'My grace is sufficient for you, for My strength is made perfect in weakness.' Therefore most gladly I will boast in my weaknesses, that the power of Christ may rest upon me" (2 Cor. 12:8–9).

Some scholars say Paul's thorn in the flesh was a debilitating illness, while others argue that it was a malicious person—a messenger of Satan hell-bent on tormenting him. It's a moot point because we are focusing on Paul's persistence. God was silent the first two times he prayed. Paul had no idea where God stood on the issue. Whether his prayers were in vain or outside the scope of God's will was unclear to him. His repeated prayers were just an adult-sized version of asking: "God, are You OK?" God was silent even after two times of pleading the same request.

But God was OK. His silence schooled Paul. God's silence taught Paul to practice persistence—a quality everyone needs to have a powerful prayer life. Paul learned the lesson and persisted in prayer because he knew the value of divine pursuit and unwavering courage.

Paul's persistence was steeped in faith. He had a bold trust in God's willingness to answer him. At the end of Paul's third request God spoke. The answer may not have been what Paul wanted to hear, but it brought him to a place of peace. God's answer was so medicinal that it didn't matter if the thorn was removed or not. Paul was changed. The Lord showed him that when he's weak, Christ is strong within him. Paul's victory was his becoming more dependent on God in the face of adversity. Persistence in prayer brought out this revelation. He did not let God's initial silence deter him from praying.

Your child must learn similar lessons! The silence of God is God's way of saying: "Pursue Me! Draw closer to Me! Don't back away! Get fired up about building a deeper relationship with Me!" The silence of God is not meant to provoke you to anger or make you conclude that your needs are unimportant to God. His silence is a time for renewing your passion for a deeper communion with Him.

GOD IS GOOD

Before saying grace that morning, four-year-old Lois prayed, "Dear God, I don't think anybody could be a better God. Well, I just want You to know that I am not just saying that because You are God already." At such a tender age this little girl was able to draw the conclusion that God is good. And she wanted to register her opinion. Gratitude toward God is an important ingredient in prayer. This is what Erika and Joshua taught their children very early in their spiritual formation. As her kids looked on, Erika used to pray in a very simple way. Her goal was to model to them that prayer was simple, but simple does not mean useless or unimportant. She always started her prayers with thanks, praise, and appreciation to God.

This modeling bolstered the children's courage to start praying themselves by first being thankful. They learned that before making a request of God, they should thank Him for His goodness. At first Erika would feed them one or two things to thank God for. She piled on tons of encouragement after they voiced their thankful phrases. Their confidence concerning prayer soared. They soon began thanking God for their friends, family members, and sometimes even their toys and pets.

This couple's demonstration of prayer is totally different than what six-year-old Manny says about his mom. Manny quietly confessed once, "My mom talks to God when we need more money."

Don't slip into that bad habit. Giving thanks is the password into God's presence. Fanny Crosby, the great hymn writer, modeled thankfulness even for her loss of sight at the young age of six. Crosby says: "If perfect earthly sight were offered me tomorrow I would not accept it. I might not have sung hymns to the praise of God if I had been distracted by the beautiful and interesting things about me."[3] The point I'm making is that gratitude and praise should be a foundational element of our prayer life.

Jesus taught us how to structure our prayers. Praise precedes requests! He said that we should pray: "Our Father who is in heaven, *hallowed* be Your name"

(Matt. 6:9, emphasis added). The word *hallowed* means "holy." In prayer, when we describe or list an attribute of God, such as His holiness, it's a form of praising Him. This is not empty flattery. God is not on an ego trip. We're actually telling God that we are aware of His goodness, and for that we are most thankful.

You are supposed to enter into His courts with praise and honor (Ps. 100:4). Praise should precede your prayer requests.

Several years ago I started a ministry called the School of Prayer. My vision is to increase the knowledge and proficiency of prayer in the body of Christ. We offer three levels of instruction: beginner, intermediate, and advanced. Those who graduate to the advanced course learn how to teach others the art of prayer. These graduates usually become the prayer leaders of their local churches. I firmly believe that successful prayer leaders develop others into effective intercessors. Among the topics we teach them is the *path of prayer.* In other words, how does the Bible give us the road map for prayer?

There are four distinct steps or movements when we pray. You begin with *praise* and move to *purify.* From there you go on to *pray,* where the bulk of your time is spent, and then conclude with *praise.* This may seem choppy and mechanical, but it's much like dancing. When you see skilled dancers, the individual steps within the dance are invisible to the untrained. The dancers gracefully glide from one movement to the next. So effortless and smooth are the routines that you would never imagine that there are distinctly choreographed steps to the dance. The same is true of a seasoned intercessor's prayers.

The experienced intercessors enter God's courts with praise and then ask Him to purify them, which is done through confession and repentance of sin. After that they move on to the primary reason for their visit to the throne room—to pray. Before you leave the King, having made a plea and a petition of Him, you must offer thanks. This is where the final praise of God occurs. You cannot leave the King's presence without thanking Him for hearing and answering your request.

Take a closer look at the prayers in the Bible, and you'll notice how they are sandwiched with praise and gratitude. The Lord's Prayer had it (Matt. 6:9–13), and Paul's model prayer in his letter to the Ephesians showed it (Eph. 1:15–21). Even the apostles' prayers, offered on the heels of public embarrassment by jealous religious rulers, reflected this four-part structure (Acts 4:23–31).

The goodness of God calls for gratitude! This is why the Bible says: "Give to the LORD the glory due His name" (1 Chron. 16:29). Gratitude should always saturate our prayers. God is too good to be underappreciated.

GOD FORGIVES

Some people stop praying because they struggle with forgiveness. They are unable to forgive themselves for something they may have done. They might even get tripped up over the hurtful actions of others toward them. They wrestle with the need to forgive that person. Six-year-old Debbie prayed, "Dear God, did You really mean 'do unto others as they do unto you'? Because if you did, then I'm going to fix my brother." Her cute little prayer revealed the struggle of her heart—forgiveness.

Jesus taught that our prayers cannot be answered if we don't forgive those who hurt us (Matt. 6:15). This is a critical lesson for your children to learn. Since God is so free in His willingness to forgive us, we must follow suit. At first kids may struggle with the need to forgive their friends or siblings because they are angry with them. Don't dismiss their resentment. Their feelings and emotions are real and important, just as your anger toward those who've hurt you is real and important. Take a creative approach so that the necessity of forgiving others is seen, understood, and never to be forgotten by your child.

Consider playing the forgiveness game. Explain that when forgiveness is not extended, it becomes a weight they carry on their shoulders. The pain caused by their friend or whomever becomes heavy every time they think about it. And each time someone else does something wrong to them, it adds to the other emotional junk they are already carrying. It weighs them down.

From either a seated or standing position, give your child something to carry for a few feet. Each item you place on their shoulders or in their hands represents something that someone did to them and they've not forgiven. Start by adding something light on their shoulders and have them walk ten feet out and back. Ask them if it is heavy. Most likely they'll say, "No." Then ask, "How would you like to carry that around with you all the time?" At that, add something heavier, perhaps a book in their hand, and have them walk the original distance out and back. Again you should ask, "How would you like to carry this stuff around all the time?"

Let them know that each time they ask God to help them forgive their friend for what he did to them, the weight of that pain is lifted from their shoulder. Then take one item away. Since there are other things still on their shoulders or in their hand, ask, "Would you like to walk around like this even though the weight is lighter?" They will certainly say, "No!" Work the example so that it's a memorable experience and a rich teaching moment.

Make the exercise fun and funny. It will help them better understand forgiveness. It also simulates the importance of God's great forgiveness of us. He never wants us to walk around with heavy burdens that make life difficult and cumbersome. The main point of the forgiveness exercise is for your child to know that if they don't forgive those who hurt them, God is not able to answer their prayers.

GOD IS CREATIVE

"Dear God, did you mean for the giraffe to look like that, or was it an accident?" Norma prayed. This preschooler was really trying to wrap her mind around the question: Is being different a bad thing? Children need to know that God is a creative genius. He made all of us look differently, walk differently, talk differently, and even possess different gifts. God did this because He finds pleasure in our differences. They please Him! The quicker they learn this lesson, the more comfortable they will be with themselves and the more open they'll be to celebrating their uniqueness.

Do you remember when you had to baby proof your home so your babies would not hurt themselves? You were so thoughtful and thorough because of the importance of the project. Well, this project of gift identification is just as important. The childproofing stage lasts a few years. But the gift identification is one that will serve your child for a lifetime. The psalmist writes: "I will praise you, for You made me with fear and wonder; marvelous are Your works, and You know me completely" (Ps. 139:14).

Help your children discover their personality, gifts, likes, and dislikes. Each discovery should be celebrated because they have been wonderfully and uniquely made by God. Comparing them with another takes away from the beauty of God's creation and creativity. He wanted them to be different from their sibling. Their creativity, once highlighted, should strengthen them when it comes to prayer. Rather than holding back and questioning the creativity of God as Norma did about the giraffe, your child will know to go boldly before the throne of grace when it's time to pray.

I have a family in my congregation who taught their two children how to become comfortable with their gifts. The dad asked the two kids to identify problems in their midst and discover creative ways to solve them. One morning the mother dropped nine-year-old Joey off at school one morning, and she noticed an extra backpack in the car. When she questioned Joey, he nonchalantly said he noticed a kid in his school whose backpack had broken a couple of weeks earlier. When he questioned him about it, the little boy said that his parents couldn't afford a new one.

Joey took it upon himself to solve the problem by giving the boy one of his two backpacks. The mother made a huge deal about Joey's compassion. It was not something that was forced or surfaced because of parental pressure. His empathy for the classmate was an indicator of how God had uniquely fashioned him.

His younger sister, Lizzie, at eight years old, discovered that she had different gifts. She was naturally wired with leadership and administrative gifts. Her mom, a consultant to nonprofit organizations, had a client that ran a homeless shelter. While mother and daughter were running a few errands, the mom decided to stop by the shelter to finish up a conversation with her client. Lizzie didn't want to wait in the car. Once inside, the mom pointed her to the playroom where the kids who lived at the shelter hung out. To Lizzie's dismay the toys were not the greatest.

Without any conversation with her parents, Lizzie approached the executive director of the neighborhood Boys and Girls Club—the place she and Joey frequented after school—and asked if it would be possible for her entire class to drop off new and gently used toys there. The toys would be earmarked for the kids at the homeless shelter. The executive director called Lizzie's mom to let her know what was happening. The Boys and Girls Club got behind the project, and their families donated toys as well. When it was all said and done, eight large boxes of toys were delivered to the kids of the homeless shelter. This happened because eight-year-old Lizzie saw a problem and did something about it.

Make much of your children's strengths. God has wired them with unique creativity, perspective, and abilities that make them excel at certain things. Conversely, help them make sense of their weaknesses. There are two categories. The first reflects the things no one can change, while the second provide them an opportunity for personal development. The things that cannot be changed ought to be accepted the same way a birthmark is accepted—as a unique stamp of God. The other, the category of weaknesses, can become exciting projects of prayer and growth.

GOD WANTS RELATIONSHIP

Children ought to have a growing relationship with God that is built on honesty, authenticity, and obedience. God's love for us never wavers! It never increases or decreases based on how we behave—good or bad. It's constant. God is love. Period. But a necessary point of clarity in their spiritual formation must be learning how their behavior toward God and people can adversely affect the outcome of their prayers. Peter pointed out this principle as he drew an example from the area of marriage. He writes: "Likewise, you husbands, live considerately with your wives, giving honor to the woman as the weaker vessel, since they too are also heirs of the grace of life, so that your prayers will not be hindered" (1 Pet. 3:7).

There is no question that the husband referred to in this verse loves his wife. The problem is that he's not behaving in a loving way toward her. The all-knowing God observes and is forced to turn a deaf ear to the husband's prayers. Regardless of his sincerity, faith, or prayerfulness, his behavior toward his wife affects his relationship with God. Although God wants to answer his prayers, their relationship has become strained because the husband is not honoring his wife.

This example is not a one-sided one. The same outcome would easily be the case if the wife was treating her husband disrespectfully, a child his parent, a parent his child, or a sibling their brother or sister. The point that Peter was sharing is that our mistreatment of one another forces God to become silent toward our prayers. In this instance the silence of God is no indication that God isn't OK. Rather, it's showing a breakdown in a human relationship, which bothers God. His silence says: "Fix it! Ask for forgiveness! Hold out the olive branch."

A little boy named Billy went to his mother demanding a new bicycle. His mother decided that she should have him take a good look deep down on the inside and inspect himself because he'd been behaving like a brat. And so she said, "Well, Billy, it's not Christmas and it's not your birthday, and we don't have the money to give you to buy whatever you want to buy whenever you want to buy it. So why don't you write a letter to Jesus and pray that *He* will give you a bicycle?"

After his temper tantrum, which included throwing himself down and kicking his feet on the floor, Billy got up and stormed out of the room. He went to his own room and started writing his letter to Jesus. "Dear Jesus," he wrote. "I've been a good boy this year, and I would appreciate a new bicycle. Signed, Your friend, Billy."

Now Billy realized that Jesus knew what kind of boy he'd been the whole year. He'd been misbehaving and disobedient. So after thinking about that for a minute, Billy ripped up the letter and gave it another try. This time he wrote, "Dear Jesus, I've been an OK boy this year and I want a new bicycle. Signed, Yours truly, Billy."

Well, knowing that this letter wasn't totally honest either, Billy tore it up and tried again. "Dear Jesus," it went, "I've *thought* about being a good boy this year, and can I have a new bicycle? Signed, Billy."

Finally, realizing that this still wasn't right, Billy looked deep down in his heart to try to understand what his mother was saying. He walked out of his room and out of the house and wandered around his neighborhood. Suddenly he found himself in front of the local Catholic church. So he went inside and saw the altar up front. He wanted to go up there and kneel down, but it had been so long since he'd prayed that he felt that God wouldn't want to hear from him. So he just thought longer about how he'd been acting and continued to look deep down in his heart.

Finally he got so frustrated he turned around to walk out of the church. On his way out he noticed all these statues around. Seeing a little one, he snatched it up and ran out of the church as fast as he could. He ran to his house and put the statue under his bed. Then he started praying.

"Jesus!" He said breathlessly. "Jesus! I got Your mama! If You don't give me a bicycle, You'll never see her again! Signed, You know who!"

We can't recommend that as an example of building a healthy relationship with God, can we? Sometimes we try to push God to do things in ways that just aren't in keeping with His character or what He requires of ours. God wants us to act with a good deal of honesty, authenticity, and obedience, more than little Billy did.

Whenever we feel like praying, "God, are You OK?," it means that it's high time for us to inspect ourselves. The fact of the matter is that *we* might not be OK spiritually, emotionally, or relationally. God's silence gives us time to get ourselves together. Repentance gives us an opportunity to wipe the slate of our lives clean.

A Sunday school teacher once asked a class what was meant by the word *repentance*. A little boy put up his hand and said, "It is being sorry for your sins." A little girl also raised her hand and said, "Please, it is being sorry enough to quit."[4] God's pardon is always available to people who humble themselves and repent of their sins.

Action Steps

Kids have been divinely wired to ask interesting questions about God. Don't ignore them. Try to answer as many of their questions as possible because it will help them in their spiritual formation.

The silence of God provides you with an opportunity that words may never provide. You gain courage, faith, and passion to further pursue the Lord during moments where He's silent.

Here are some action steps you can take with your child:

- Since God takes pleasure in being creative, consider playing a little game with your children to help them discover their own creativity. Ask them to tell you the name of five funny-looking foods that taste good. Then ask them to tell you five funny things about themselves. Then tell them why each one of those funny things are unique and good.

- After you finish playing the creative game, pray with your child something like this:

Lord, thank You for how You made my child unique. She reflects Your creativity. May we always celebrate her uniqueness. Thank You for placing her into our family. I pray this in Jesus's name. Amen.

CONCLUSION

———— ✹ ————

O NE OF THE greatest legacies you can ever leave
your children is a strong prayer life. Once they
are introduced to the Savior, the next best thing in your
children's spiritual formation is knowing firsthand how
to access Him through prayer. Powerful praying is when
we dare to believe God for His miracle-working strength
to go to work on our behalf.

There is an old story about a pastor of the neighborhood church and a kitten. As he and his kids were playing
with the kitten, it climbed up a tree in his backyard and
was afraid to come down. The pastor coaxed and coaxed,
offering warm milk and holding out his hands for the
kitten to jump. Nothing worked. The tree was not sturdy
enough to climb, so the pastor decided that if he tied a
rope to his car and drove away so that the tree bent down,
his kids could reach up and get the kitten.

He did all this, checking his progress in the car frequently, and then figured if he went just a little bit

farther, the tree would be bent sufficiently for the kids to grab the kitten. But as he moved the car forward a little further, the rope broke.

The tree went *boing!*, and the kitten instantly sailed through the air—out of sight. The pastor felt terrible.

He walked all over the neighborhood asking people if they'd seen a little kitten. No. Nobody had seen a stray kitten.

So he prayed, "Lord, I just commit this kitten to Your keeping," and went on about his business. A few days later he was at the grocery store and met one of his church members.

He happened to look into her shopping cart and was amazed to see cat food.

Now this woman was a cat hater, and everyone knew it, so he asked her, "Why are you buying cat food when you hate cats so much?"

She replied, "You won't believe this…" She then told him how her little girl had been begging her for a kitten, but she kept refusing. Then a few days before, the child had begged again, so the Mom finally told her little girl, "Well, if God gives you a kitten, I'll let you keep it."

She told the pastor, "I watched my child go out in the yard, get on her knees, and ask God for a kitten.

"And really, Pastor, you won't believe this, but I saw it with my own eyes.

"A kitten suddenly came flying out of the clear blue sky, with its paws outspread, and landed right in front of her."[1]

Although this story is fictitious, it does accurately illustrate that praying kids are not deterred from engaging God in every area of their lives. This is how prayer and spiritual formation should be viewed. Prayer is practical. Prayer should touch all aspects of your life. Your job is to pray. God's job is to perform the miracle.

I pray that God gives you tremendous success in helping your children become skilled in the art of prayer.

PRAYER EXERCISES

———— ✸ ————

CHILDREN OFTEN LEARN important concepts and valuable habits through fun activities. Prayer can be introduced the same way. Based on the age and maturity of your child, consider using any of these activities, in part or whole, to raise them to know how to pray.

TEXT A PRAYER

Your child's era is a social media one. In order for prayer to be meaningful and relevant, you must show them how it fits into their world. Consider having them use your phone or another's to send a prayer text to a relative. For example:

- **Christian relative:** "Hi, Grandma. This morning I prayed for you by asking, 'Heavenly Father, help Grandma to not be lonely but to have a lot of good friends and

for our relationship to become stronger.' I
can't wait to see you!"

- **A non-Christian relative:** "Hi, Grandma.
  This morning I prayed for you by asking,
  'Loving God, help Grandma to experience
  Your love in a greater way. Please answer
  all of her spiritual questions and bless her
  in a big way. I ask You this in the name
  of my Savior, Jesus. Amen.' I love you,
  Grandma. See you soon!"

Tweet a Prayer

Twitter is a great way to connect with and influence a lot
of people. Consider taking a selfie with your child and
post it alongside of his prayer. Since Twitter presently
limits you to 140 characters, your child's prayer should
be focused and simple. God is not limited by space, distance, or the vehicle we use to offer our prayers. Who
knows, your child's prayers may go viral. This is not an
attempt to be cute. It is using kid power in a contemporary way to bring the needs of the broader society to
Jesus. Remember to share with your child the response
of the tweets your followers post about his prayers. This
will be most encouraging.

Sing a Prayer

Singing is a great way to teach your child how to pray.
The Book of Psalms is God's songbook and is filled

with the prayers of psalmists like David, Solomon, and the sons of Korah. Choose one of the psalms and sing a few verses together. For example, Psalm 145:1–2 (NIV) provides us with language that little kids love to hear. It says:

> I will exalt you, my God the King; I will praise your name for ever and ever. Every day I will praise you and extol your name for ever and ever.

Add gestures and movement to match key words, and you'll have your little one jumping around as they sing their prayers to God. For example, some words that can easily have fun gestures are as follows:

- **Exalt (verse 1):** This word means to raise above everything else. Your child needs to exalt God above everything else in his life. Have him tell you something that he really values; perhaps this is a toy or an activity. Then say, "God wants to be more important (exalted) than this toy (or activity)." Have your child raise his or her hands every time the word *exalt* is sung.

- **Every day (verse 2):** These words capture the ongoing praise your child should have toward God's blessings. Your child needs to praise God *every day* for something. Ask her, "What are you thankful for?" The answer should be inserted into the prayer song. If her answer is, "I'm thankful for my mommy and daddy," then the prayer song should go something like this: "Lord, every day I will praise You for Mommy and Daddy." Have her jump up and down every time she sings the words *every day*.

WORSHIP

Music is an excellent way to get little kids engaged in spiritual activities. Get a few kid-friendly worship songs that have powerful lyrics. Spend a few minutes in worship together. Consider dancing before the Lord, even lifting your hands to heaven, as a sign of a surrendered heart. Explain the meaning of your actions. For example, dancing means that you're thankful and happy for God's forgiveness, love, and blessings. (See Psalm 30:11; 149:3; 150:4.) Here are some prayers to pray with your children after worship:

- After the song ends, choose a couple of the phrases in the lyrics and let them be a springboard to your child's prayers.

- Pray for the artists who wrote the song. Ask God to raise up powerful artists who will write songs that will lead many people to Jesus.

STARTING WELL

A great day starts off with prayer. Help your child to look ahead and envision the kind of day it will be. If there are fun activities or trips scheduled, the prayer will capture that. If there are stressful things to do, such as going to the doctor, taking a test at school, or a long list of chores, the prayers will take that into consideration. Here are some examples of prayers:

- **Fun day ahead:** "Dear God, thank You for the fun day we have planned. Help me to learn a lot and laugh a lot. I want to learn how to be brave and smart. I want to laugh because laughing is good. Use me to cheer up someone else today. I pray this in Jesus's name. Amen."

- **Stressful day ahead:** "Dear God, fill my heart with peace. Walk with me throughout the day so that I will have courage and strength. Use me to help others know of Your peace. I pray this in Jesus's name. Amen."

FINISHING WELL

Every day should end in prayer. Whether this practice occurs before or after you read a story to your child, raise them to start and end their day in prayer. This will help your child to see God as an integral part of life. Here are some examples of prayers:

- **Reflecting on the day:** "Dear God, thank You for this great day that You gave me. I had a lot of fun. Help me to continue to grow in wisdom and obedience."

- **The family:** "Heavenly Father, I thank You for my mom and dad. Give them strength to provide for our family. May every need that we have be met! Help us to love each other deeply."

PRAYER BY HEIGHT

Little kids are very observant. Use their natural bent as a fun way to have them pray for people in their lives based on the person's height. One day have them pray for those in their life, starting from the tallest to the shortest person. The next day reverse the order—the shortest to the tallest person is the order of their prayers.

FIVE-FINGER PRAYER

The five-finger prayer has become rather popular in children's circles. Have your child hold out one hand. Each finger from the thumb to the pinky can be used to represent someone in their life. For example:

- **The thumb:** Pray for someone close to them—perhaps a family member.

- **The index finger:** Say a prayer for someone who points them in the right direction. This can be a school teacher, a babysitter, or a Sunday school teacher.

- **The middle finger:** Pray for someone who is in a significant position of leadership, like the president of our country, your governor, or your pastor.

- **The ring finger:** Say a prayer for a kid who is having family problems. Perhaps his mom and dad are experiencing marriage problems. Pray for the healing of their relationship.

- **The pinky finger:** Pray for a friend and for himself.

PRAYER BOARD

To help your child visualize specific things he wants to pray about, get a large poster board, magic markers, glue, and crayons. Together, clip out pictures that represent his topic of prayer from an old magazine or newspaper, or print them from the Internet, and glue them onto the poster board. You can label them. Once completed, the board will represent things that your child is praying for.

Prayer for the Nations

Your child needs to know that God loves the world. To make that practical, take a globe or locate a world map on the Internet. Show him where he is on the map explaining that God loves everybody everywhere. Invite him to pray for people in different countries. Here are some examples:

- **Nation of origin:** If you or a grandparent was born in another country, show it to your child on the map. Then pray for that nation to prosper and that the people may accept Jesus as their Savior.

- **Kids of that nation:** Have your child to pray for all the children the same age as her in that specific nation she's selected.

Family Photo Prayers

In order to get your children in the habit of praying for their family, pull out a family photo album. Pray for the people who appear in the pictures on each page. You may make this activity as short or as long as they can stay engaged. Even if there are family members whom you've not seen in a while because of conflict, invite your children to pray for the healing of the relationship. This will help them see that conflict is not a good reason to stop praying for a person. It will also bring them to the reality that God cares about our building an emotionally healthy family.

CELL PHONE PRAYERS

Your cell phone contains a wealth of things that your child can help you pray about. Here are a few options:

- Pull up the list of your "favorites"—the people with whom you often speak with on the phone. You and your child can go down the list praying for each one, one at a time.

- Pull up the last ten or twenty photos you've taken, and pray for the people seen in each one.

WALK AND PRAY

One of the great heroes of the Bible used to walk while he prayed. Elisha the prophet is shown walking back and forth in his room as he prayed for a child (2 Kings 4:32–35). Turn this into a fun activity by writing powerful words on an index card. Each card has one word. Place the cards a short distance from one another on the floor. Words like obedience, praise, school, mom, or dad can appear on the card. Or write down whatever theme you'd like to see become integrated into your child's prayers.

You can have worship music playing softly in the background to help create a mood for praying. Explain the prayer game to your child, demonstrating how you can pray about a theme every time you step on the card bearing that label. Your child can stand on a card as long or short as he wants. But each card he walks to should be the topic of his prayer.

LISTENING PRAYER

Since prayer is a dialogue and not a monologue, you should strive to teach this aspect of prayer to your child. Ask your child to tell you about her favorite game. While she's excitedly talking, interrupt her without any prompting. Ask her, "How did you like it when I interrupted you?" Most likely she'll say, "I didn't like it. It's not nice."

Then say, "This is what we do if we're the ones doing all of the talking when we're in prayer." In other words, "You must stop praying for a while so that God can speak to your heart." Listening prayer is when you've prayed for a few minutes and then become silent. Your silence means that you're listening for God to speak. If you're praying constantly, it means you're interrupting God as He tries to speak.

THE FORGIVENESS PRAYER

Here's one I mentioned in chapter 9.

When you don't forgive someone, the weight of the hurt they have caused you weighs you down. Equally, if not more importantly, when you don't forgive others, God doesn't forgive you (Matt. 6:15). From either a seated or standing position, give your child something to carry for a few feet. Each item you place on her shoulders or in her hands represents something that someone did to her that she has not forgiven. Start by adding something light on her shoulders and have her walk ten feet out and back.

Ask her, "How would you like to carry that around with you all the time?" Then add something heavier, perhaps a book in her hand, and have her walk the original distance out and back. Again you should ask, "How would you like to carry this stuff around all the time?" Make the exercise fun and funny.

Let her know that each time she asks God to help her forgive her friend for what she did to her, the weight of that pain is lifted from her shoulders. Then take one item away. Since there are other things still on her shoulders or in her hand, ask, "Would you like to walk around like this even though the weight is lighter?" She will certainly say, "No!" Work the example so that it's a memorable experience.

Ask her if there's anything bothering her that must be prayed for. If forgiveness must be extended, have her pray, "God, help me to forgive XYZ person, who has hurt me. Take the burden off my shoulders. In Jesus's name. Amen." As a parent, you then determine if a conversation must follow with your child and the person who was the center of their request for forgiveness.

THE EVERYWHERE PRAYER

To engage your child in a broader aspect of prayer, use the everywhere prayer as a tool. You will teach them how to pray up, out, in, down, and all around—the five directions of prayer.

- **Up:** Looking up to God, your child can pray: "Lord, help me to grow closer to You and serve You better."

- **Out:** This speaks of having stronger relationships with others. Pray, "Lord, help me to build strong friendships with people in my school, church, and neighborhood."

- **In:** This direction speaks of the child's inner life. Teach him to pray for himself by asking, "God, help me to be brave, wise, and caring. I want to be a great follower of Jesus and a great lover of people."

- **Down:** Looking down speaks of people who are hurting, oppressed, or poor. This teaches your child to pray for justice, compassion, and mercy for the poor and oppressed among us. Have him ask, "God, help me to have compassion and mercy for people who are hurting. I ask that You will

provide food for the hungry and homes
for the homeless. Raise up people who
will help the hurting, in the name of Jesus.
Amen."

* **All around:** Have your child spin around
  with his pointing finger out. This symbol-
  izes the world. Invite your child to pray,
  "Lord, let Your love and blessings touch the
  world. Raise up missionaries to spread the
  message of Jesus everywhere. Provide water
  and medicine to people around the world."

THE LORD'S PRAYER

Memorize the Lord's Prayer. It provides a rich structure and an invaluable content to prayer. Millions of
Christians learned this prayer in their childhood. Explore
creative methods to help your child to memorize:

> Our Father who is in heaven, hallowed be Your
> name. Your kingdom come; Your will be done on
> earth, as it is in heaven. Give us this day our daily
> bread. And forgive us our debts, as we forgive
> our debtors. And lead us not into temptation, but
> deliver us from evil.
>
> —MATTHEW 6:9–13

As you ask the Lord to give you creative ideas that
can engage your child in prayer, He will. This is not an
exhaustive list; it just helps prime your creative pump.

NOTES

———— ☼ ————

Introduction

1.   Dan Brewster, "The '4/14 Window': Child Ministries and Mission Strategies," Compassion International, updated August 2005, accessed April 26, 2016, http://www.compassion.com/multimedia/The%204_14%20Window.pdf.

Chapter 1
The Power of a Praying Parent

1.   Dick Eastman, *No Easy Road* (Fairfax, VA: Chosen Books, 1973).

2.   E. M. Bounds, *Purpose in Prayer* (Grand Rapids, MI: Baker Book House, 1978), 48.

3.   Dick Eastman, *The Hour That Changes the World* (Fairfax, VA: Chosen Books, 2002), 21.

4.   "Rick Warren," AZ Quotes, accessed February 13, 2016, http://www.azquotes.com/quote/1458207.

5.   Rebecca Lamar Harmon, *Susanna: Mother of the Wesleys* (Nashville: Abingdon Press, 1968), 60.

6.   "Mark Batterson," AZ Quotes, accessed February 13, 2016, http://www.azquotes.com/quote/895123.

7.   "Inflight Passenger Announcements," AirOdyssey.net, accessed February 2, 2016, http://airodyssey.net/reference/inflight/#takeoff.

8.   Alexander Whyte, "The Magnificence of Prayer," News for Christians, accessed February 29, 2016, http://www.newsforchristians.com/clser1/whyte_005.html.

9.   "Mark Batterson," AZ Quotes, accessed February 13, 2016, http://www.azquotes.com/quote/762388.

10.   Wesley E. Duewel, *Heroes of the Holy Life* (Grand Rapids, MI: Zondervan, 2002), 100.

11.   Michael Lipka, "What Surveys Say About Worship Attendance—and Why Some Stay Home," Pew Research Center, accessed February 2, 2016, http://www.pewresearch.org/fact-tank/2013/09/13/what-surveys-say-about-worship-attendance-and-why-some-stay-home/.

12.   Alan Hirsch, *The Forgotten Ways* (Ada, MI: Brazos Press, 2006), 85.

13.   "Only One With Hand Up," Bible.org, accessed April 4, 2016, https://bible.org/illustration/only-one-hand.

CHAPTER 2
THE POWER OF A PRAYING CHILD

1.   James S. Hewett, ed., *Illustrations Unlimited* (Wheaton, IL: Tyndale House Publishers, 1988), 116–117.

2.   Kathryn Lay, "A Little Girl's Answered Prayer," *Guideposts*, accessed February 2, 2016, https://www.guideposts.org/faith-in-daily-life/prayer/answered-prayers/a-little-girls-answered-prayer?nopaging=1.

3.   Muhammad Ali's Twitter, accessed February 24, 2016, https://twitter.com/muhammadali/status/302446833022668801.

4.   G. Curtis Jones, *1000 Illustrations for Preaching and Teaching* (Nashville: Broadman Press, 1986), 297.

5.   Donald O. Clifton and Paula Nelson, "How 'Average' People Excel," *Reader's Digest*, 1992.

6.   Howard and Geraldine Taylor, *Hudson Taylor's Spiritual Secret* (New Kensington, PA: Whitaker House, 2003), 32–33.

7.   Duewel, *Heroes of the Holy Life*, 92.

8.   J. H. Jowett, *God—Our Contemporary* (New York: Fleming H. Revell Co., 1922), 18.

CHAPTER 3
JESUS–THE FIRST TWELVE YEARS

1.   Nicole Pelletiere, "Parents Capture Toddler's Prayer on Baby Monitor," *Good Morning America*, January 26, 2016,

accessed January 27, 2016, https://gma.yahoo.com/parents
-capture-toddlers-prayer-baby-monitor-165430365--abc-news
-lifestyle.html?nwltr=gma_fb#.

2.   Oswald Chambers, *My Utmost for His Highest* (Grand
Rapids, MI: Discovery House Publishers, 1989).

3.   William Douglas Chamberlain, *The Meaning of Repentance* (Philadelphia: Westminster Press, 1943), 23.

4.   Dave Clark, "Treat Each Other Like the Answer to a
Prayer," Ankeny Christian Church, Sermon Central, December
2012, accessed April 12, 2016, http://www.sermoncentral.com
/illustrations/sermon-illustration-dave-clark-stories-prayerof
faith-82557.asp.

CHAPTER 4

LITTLE JOHNNY (A.K.A. JOHN THE BAPTIST)

1.   Hewett, ed., *Illustrations Unlimited*, 115.

2.   Joachim Jeremias, *Jerusalem in the Time of Jesus* (Philadelphia: Fortress Press, 1969), 200–201.

3.   Hewett, ed., *Illustrations Unlimited*, 421.

4.   A. W. Tozer, *Of God and Men* (Chicago: Moody Publishers, 2015), 124.

5.   Dick Eastman, *The Purple Pig and Other Miracles*
(Lake Mary, FL: Charisma House Publishers, 2010), 38.

6.   Scott Clement, "Americans Continue to Pray Even as
Religious Practices Wither, Survey Finds," *Washington Post*,
March 6, 2015, accessed February 23, 2016, https://www
.washingtonpost.com/local/americans-continue-to-pray-even
-as-religious-practices-wither-survey-finds/2015/03/06/89cbb
99a-c37f-11e4-9271-610273846239_story.html.

7.   Richard Foster, *Celebration of Discipline* (San Francisco: HarperSanFrancisco, 1988), 97.

8.   Ruth Haley Barton, *Strengthening the Soul of Your
Leadership* (Downers Grove, IL: InterVarsity Press, 2008), 22.

9.   "Henri Nouwen," AZ Quotes, accessed February 13,
2016, http://www.azquotes.com/quote/1302165.

Chapter 5
Unlocking Kid Power

1.   David Cerqueira, "A Dying Girl Shows Honor of Serving God," *Christianity Today*, Preachingtoday.com, adapted from *Evangel* magazine (December 2005), accessed March 1, 2016, http://www.christianity.com/11622768/.

2.   "John Vianney," AZ Quotes, accessed February 13, 2016, http://www.azquotes.com/quote/550399.

3.   Silas Shotwell, "What Are You Good For?" Sermon Search.com, originally published in *Homemade* in 1987, accessed February 1, 2016, http://www.sermonsearch.com /sermon-illustrations/7437/what-are-you-good-for/.

4.   "Finished a Day of Teaching, 'a Day Wasted,'" History tech.Wordpress.com, April 12, 2010, accessed April 4, 2016, https://historytech.wordpress.com/2010/04/12/finished-a-day -of-teaching-a-day-wasted/.

5.   *Sunday School Times*, as viewed at Sermons.org, "Mothers, Cares of," accessed May 25, 2016, http://www .sermons.org/mothers.html.

Chapter 6
Add Faith to Your Prayers

1.   "Saint Augustine Quotes," BrainyQuote.com, accessed April 7, 2016, http://www.brainyquote.com/quotes/quotes/s /saintaugus121380.html.

2.   Ken Auletta, "The Lost Tycoon," *New Yorker*, April 23, 2001, accessed March 1, 2016, http://www.newyorker.com /magazine/2001/04/23/the-lost-tycoon.

3.   "Bringing a Little Humor to Your Mother's Day," Grow Counseling, May 11, 2012, accessed April 8, 2016, http://www .growcounseling.com/bringing-humor-mothers-day/.

4.   "African Woman's Prayer of Faith," PreachingToday. com, accessed May 12, 2016, http://www.preachingtoday.com/ illustrations/2005/december/16259.html. Used with permission.

5.   Blair Justice, *Who Gets Sick: Thinking and Health* (Houston, TX: Peak Press, 1987), 301.

6.   Linda Byron, KING-TV, Seattle, "Once a Shelter Dog, Now He's Saving Lives," USA Today, December 1, 2015, accessed February 3, 2016, http://www.usatoday.com/story /news/humankind/2015/11/30/these-shelter-dogs-turning-into -police-super-stars/76572992/.

7.   Francis A. Schaeffer, *How Should We Then Live? The Rise and Decline of Western Thought and Culture* (Wheaton, IL: Crossway, L'Abri 50th Anniversary Edition, 2005), 24.

8.   Steve May, *The Story File: 1001 Contemporary Illustrations for Speakers, Writers and Preachers* (Peabody, MA: Hendrickson Publishers, 2000), 19.

9.   Fox Butterfield, "Pornography Cited in Ouster at Harvard," *New York Times*, May 20, 1999, accessed March 1, 2016, http://www.nytimes.com/1999/05/20/us/pornography -cited-in-ouster-at-harvard.html.

10.   "Answered Prayers," 2Christ.org, accessed February 3, 2016, http://www.2christ.org/prayer/.

CHAPTER 7
PRAYING GOD'S DREAM FOR YOUR CHILD

1.   Chris Boyette and Lisa Cohen, "Sex-Trafficking Survivors Use New Ink to Reclaim Their Lives," CNN Freedom Project, September 2, 2015, accessed March 1, 2016, http:// www.cnn.com/2015/09/02/us/human-trafficking-branding -survivors-ink/index.html.

2.   Ibid.

3.   "William Carey Quotes," Brainy Quote, accessed April 8, 2016, http://www.brainyquote.com/quotes/quotes/w /williamcar191985.html.

4.   Matthew Henry, *Commentary on the Whole Bible (Concise): Exodus 32:7–14*, as seen on BibleStudyTools.com, accessed April 8, 2016, http://www.biblestudytools.com /commentaries/matthew-henry-concise/exodus/32.html.

5.   Duewel, *Heroes of the Holy Life*, 37.

6.   "Grab the First Opportunity," *Chat With God* (blog), accessed April 19, 2016, https://chatwithgod.wordpress.com /2011/03/05/grab-the-first-opportunity/.

7. "Mark Twain Quotes" Good Reads, accessed April 11, 2016, http://www.goodreads.com/quotes/404897-keep-away -from-people-who-try-to-belittle-your-ambitions.

8. Steve Almasy, "Olympian's Strength Built From Life on the Streets," CNN, February 22, 2010, accessed April 8, 2016, http://www.cnn.com/2010/SPORT/02/22/olympics.bobsledder .homeless/.

9. Ibid.

CHAPTER 8
HELP, GOD!

1. "Billy Graham Quotes," Brainy Quote, accessed April 11, 2016, http://www.brainyquote.com/quotes/quotes/b /billygraha150663.html.

2. Paul Lee Tan, *Encyclopedia of 7700 Illustrations* (Garland, TX: Bible Communications, Inc., 1996).

3. Reinhard Bonnke, *Living a Life of Fire* (Longwood, FL: Harvester Services, 2010), 78–79.

4. Ibid.

5. Anthony Perry, "Overcoming the World," Sermon Central.com, April 2009, accessed April 4, 2016, http://www .sermoncentral.com/sermons/overcoming-the-world-anthony -perry-sermon-on-action-134332.asp?Page=4.

6. David D. Ireland, "San Bernardino, Paris: When We Ask, 'Why, God?' We Are Asking the Wrong Question," FoxNews.com, December 3, 2015, accessed February 4, 2016, http://www.foxnews.com/opinion/2015/12/03/san-bernardino -paris-when-ask-why-god-are-asking-wrong-question.html.

7. "CNN Larry King Live: Interview with Joyce Meyer," CNN.com, May 19, 2005, accessed April 4, 2016, http://transcripts.cnn.com/TRANSCRIPTS/0505/19/lkl.01.html.

8. David D. Ireland, *"Failure" Is Written in Pencil* (Rockaway, NJ: Impact Publishing House, 2000), 22–23.

9. "Parenting," SermonIllustrations.com, accessed April 19, 2016, http://www.sermonillustrations.com/a-z/p/parenting.htm.

10. "James Dobson," AZ Quotes, accessed February 12, 2016, http://www.azquotes.com/quote/952000.

CHAPTER 9

GOD, ARE YOU OK?

1. G. Curtis Jones, *1000 Illustrations for Preaching and Teaching* (Nashville: Broadman Press, 1986), 293.
2. "Dwight L. Moody," AZ Quotes, accessed February 12, 2016, http://www.azquotes.com/quote/545412.
3. "Fanny Crosby," AZ Quotes, accessed February 12, 2016, http://www.azquotes.com/quote/763828.
4. Tan, *Encyclopedia of 7700 Illustrations.*

CONCLUSION

1. "Flying Kittens and Answered Prayer," John Mark Ministries, August, 28, 2003, accessed April 12, 2016, http://www .jmm.org.au/articles/1573.htm.

ABOUT THE AUTHOR

———— ✹ ————

D R. DAVID IRELAND is founder and senior pastor of Christ Church, a multisite church in northern New Jersey with an eight-thousand-member congregation of more than sixty nationalities. Diversity consultant to the National Basketball Association, Dr. Ireland leads chapel services for the New York Giants and New York Jets and at the US Pentagon. Author of approximately twenty books, Ireland has appeared on *The Dr. Phil Show*, the *CBS Evening News*, and *The 700 Club*. Through his community development corporation he offers a home for victims of domestic violence and a youth leadership institute. Rev. Ireland holds an undergraduate degree in mechanical engineering (Fairleigh Dickinson University), a graduate degree in civil engineering (Stevens Institute of Technology), and a master's degree in theology (Alliance Theological Seminary). He has an earned doctorate degree in organizational leadership (Regent University) and has completed postdoctoral work at the University of Pennsylvania. Dr. Ireland was recently appointed as a member of the Governor's Advisory Commission on Faith-Based Initiatives. He also serves on the boards of Nyack College and Alliance Theological Seminary and was an adjunct professor at Drew University. He and his wife, Marlinda, have been married since 1984 and have two adult daughters. To learn more, visit www.DavidIreland.org.

CONNECT WITH US!

CHARISMA HOUSE

(Spiritual Growth)

 Facebook.com/CharismaHouse

@CharismaHouse

Instagram.com/CharismaHouseBooks

SILOAM

(Health)

Pinterest.com/CharismaHouse

REALMS

(Fiction)

Facebook.com/RealmsFiction